DOROTHY DAY
CHAMPION OF THE POOR

by Elaine Murray Stone

Paulist Press
New York/Mahwah, N.J.

Note to the Reader

In this narrative biography, many scenes from Dorothy Day's life have been dramatized, complete with thoughts and dialogue. Though there are no footnotes within the narrative section, conversations and thoughts are based on Day's extensive written body of work. Notes have been reserved for the final chapter, which collects comments about Dorothy Day's place in the world and her likelihood of being canonized.

Cover art and interior illustrations by Patrick Kelley
Used by permission
Cover design by Lynn Else

Text copyright © 2004 by Elaine Murray Stone

Library of Congress Cataloging-in-Publication Data

Stone, Elaine Murray, 1922–
    Dorothy Day : champion of the poor / by Elaine Murray Stone.
      p. cm.
    Includes bibliographical references (p.   ).
    ISBN 0-8091-6719-0
    1. Day, Dorothy, 1897–1980. 2. Catholic—United States—Biography. 3. Social reformers—United States—Biography. I. Title.

BX4705.D283S76 2004
267'.182'092—dc22

2003025657

Published by Paulist Press
997 Macarthur Boulevard
Mahwah, New Jersey 07430

www.paulistpress.com

Printed and bound in the
United States of America

TABLE OF CONTENTS

ACKNOWLEDGMENTS

In order to write this book I needed to learn about the Catholic Worker Movement and its founders, Dorothy Day and Peter Maurin. I owe much to the many people who helped me.

I am grateful to Father Kevin Lynch, CSP, former president of Paulist Press, for suggesting that I write this book on Dorothy Day in the first place.

I am particularly indebted to Philip Runkel, archivist of the Dorothy Day-Catholic Worker Collection in the Marquette University Library in Milwaukee, Wisconsin. He very kindly read my manuscript and corrected mistakes using his vast knowledge of Dorothy Day's life and work. He also mailed me copies and originals of articles about Dorothy, including the lengthy feature article about her in a 1952 issue of *The New Yorker.*

In addition, I have been aided in my research by reference librarians Francis Marion Reid, Michael Perini, and Ellen Struzinski of the Eau Gallie Library in Melbourne, Florida.

After the research, this work could not have come to fruition without the care and assistance of my editor at Paulist Press, Susan Heyboer O'Keefe, and my typist, Cathy Gustavson.

ACKNOWLEDGMENTS

I also thank Patrick Kelley for the cover portrait of Dorothy Day and the interior illustrations, as beautiful as his artwork for all my biographies.

Last, but not least, I am also grateful to Father Douglas Bailey of the Florida Institute of Technology and to Pat McDonough, a Pulitzer Prize nominee, both of whom read the manuscript and wrote comments for the book's cover.

I hope that all those who read this story will be inspired to help the less fortunate, following the example of Dorothy Day.

Elaine Murray Stone
Melbourne, Florida
December 18, 2003

CHAPTER ONE

THE BEGINNING

The white-haired woman limped valiantly through the August heat, her square jaw set with determination. Her still-bright eyes took in the scene, glancing at the rows of grapevines on either side of the road, the brown-skinned man at her side. Dorothy Day, the internationally known Catholic activist, was marching in support of Mexican-American grape harvesters. She had flown from New York to California to march with Cesar Chavez, head of the United Farm Workers. She was seventy-five.

Mexican-American workers in California vineyards were the poorest of the poor. They spent their lives picking grapes from the vines that filled California's lush valleys. The migrant workers received little pay, no health insurance, and pitiful housing. When they had at last been organized under the United Farm Workers Union, the farm owners negotiated with the Teamsters Union to cut more favorable deals. The march through the San Joaquin Valley with Dorothy Day was planned to draw attention to their plight. Reporters gathered from all over America to record the event and take photos of the famous activists heading the parade.

DOROTHY DAY

Growing weaker by the moment, Dorothy leaned heavily on the strong arm of Cesar Chavez. She suffered from both heart trouble and crippling arthritis. Behind them walked the raggedy workers, their brown faces etched by rivulets of sweat, their worn women carrying infants and leading children.

As the marchers reached the end of the valley, a line of police officers awaited their arrival. Several vans stood by to take them to jail. Exhausted and dehydrated, Dorothy had to be carried to the police van. All the marchers, including Dorothy, were sentenced to thirty days in jail. This was nothing new to the aged activist; she had spent time locked up in New York, in Chicago, in Washington, D.C., and now in California. Each sentence had been for standing up for a cause she believed in.

As co-founder of the Catholic Worker movement, Dorothy Day had always cared about the poor and downtrodden. She spent most of her life providing food for the hungry, housing for the homeless, spiritual nourishment for her readers. And it was her work in the slums of New York that brought her prominence. She prepared and distributed meals to thousands of hungry men waiting for a handout. The food line outside the Worker house she established stretched around the block. She was also an ardent peace activist during both World War II and the Vietnam War and advised young men to avoid the draft. She participated in sit-ins and protest marches against war and compulsory air-raid drills. She was involved in the Civil Rights movement, risking her life to help Blacks in the deep South. In addition, she possessed a deep personal spirituality and started the retreat movement, hoping to increase devotion and sanctity in both priests and laity.

This range of activities, heavily centered on peace and justice, gained her both admiration and criticism. In 1999, less than twenty years after her death, New York's late Cardinal John O'Connor proposed her for initiation for canonization. Some treated the proposed canonization lightly; others were convinced of her sanctity.

Read Bain, a sociology professor and editor of *Humanist Magazine,* not only wrote in his magazine that Dorothy Day would eventually become a saint, he said the same thing to Day while she was alive. But was she really worthy of canonization, a woman whom Catholics should admire and wish to copy?

In her youth, some of her choices became a source of long-lasting sorrow and regret. But in 1926, she experienced a conversion and became a Catholic. From that day on, she no longer lived for herself but turned her life over to God.

Dorothy Day is considered the leading Catholic layperson of the twentieth century. Her autobiography, *The Long Loneliness,* published in 1952, is numbered among the one hundred best religious books of our time. How did this all come about? What should readers know about Dorothy Day's youth? Let us travel back over more than a hundred years to the beginning.

Dorothy was the middle of five children born to Grace and John Day. As both of her parents came from educated, middle-class families, Dorothy should have had a pleasant, happy childhood. But fate dealt the

Day family one blow after another, perhaps making Dorothy flexible and better prepared to face life than if she had enjoyed wealth and stability.

The Days were living in Brooklyn Heights, New York, when Dorothy was born, November 8, 1897. John Day worked as a journalist covering the Long Island horseracing circuit. Southerner by birth and blood, he carried the seeds of racial prejudice in his heart all his life. Dorothy's lovely mother, Grace Satterlee, was a northerner, born in Marlboro, New York. While attending a business school in New York City, she met and married tall, handsome John. As she'd been raised an Episcopalian, the wedding took place in a quaint Episcopal church in Greenwich Village. The Days had two sons, followed two years later by Dorothy. In 1899, her baby sister, Della, was born. Only two years apart, the girls remained close throughout their lives. They were in their teens when Mrs. Day had a fifth child, John. He was adored by both girls, who took over most of his care.

The Days lived near the beach on Long Island and had a live-in maid, so Grace had the opportunity to spend time with her little ones. In 1904, John Day was offered a position in California and the family moved to Oakland, renting a home near the Idora Park racetrack. John was able to spend time at home writing his articles. He also dreamed of turning out a novel he hoped would be made into a movie and bring the Days lots of money. But fate had something else planned.

On April 17, 1906, John Day was at the racetrack taking notes on a story for his newspaper column. He

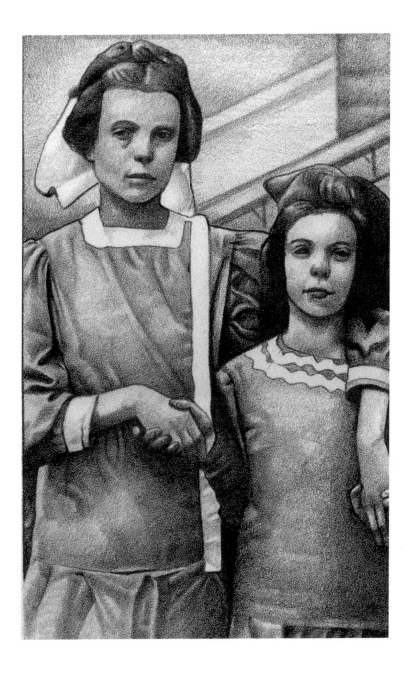

noticed that the thoroughbreds were behaving more skittishly than usual. Several horses were restless and pranced around, making it difficult for their trainers. There was something strange in the air, and the horses sensed it.

The next morning Dorothy awoke to feel her bed rolling back and forth across the room. Cracks appeared in the walls and ceiling. It was the day of the great San Francisco earthquake! Grace picked up little Della, John grabbed the boys, and Dorothy ran outside as the dining room chandelier crashed to the floor. Hanging onto their mother's skirts, the children cried and waited in the street. Where should they go? What would happen to them?

John took the ferry across the Bay to San Francisco where he discovered the city in ruins and his office burned to the ground. Having no job and fearing another tremor might do even more harm, John soon loaded his family on a train to Chicago and left the devastated area. He was sure that, with his reputation as a journalist, he would quickly find another job. The Days moved into a small apartment above a saloon in a poor area of the Windy City. John tramped the streets looking for work. He made a few dollars now and then selling articles on horseracing to magazines. At night he worked on the novel he was sure would bring the family better times. But there was no steady salary to give them security.

No longer with servants to help, Grace Day had her hands full. She fed the family cheap potatoes, bread, and vegetables, and washed the laundry by hand. She had to keep her two energetic boys quiet during the days when her husband slept. If the children made too much noise, their father would wake with a roar and frighten them.

Everything was different, and this was a difficult time for young Dorothy. But even though the Days had few possessions, their small apartment was filled with books. John Day introduced her to the great authors—Dickens, Shakespeare, Poe—the very best in literature.

Although John proclaimed himself an atheist, his wife had been raised an Episcopalian. One afternoon an Episcopal priest in the neighborhood knocked on the Days' front door. After enjoying a cup of tea with Mrs. Day, he invited the family to attend his nearby parish. After that, Grace Day and the children regularly attended Sunday services. The older boys, Sam and Donald, sang in the choir. Dorothy loved seeing them in their red cassocks and starched collars processing down the aisle. Many of the beautiful prayers from the "Book of Common Prayer" remained with her all her life, particularly the psalms, which she quoted frequently in her books and articles.

Hurt at being torn from her friends in California, Dorothy gradually made new ones in Chicago. Her closest companion was Kathryn Barrett, a Catholic. The girls often dropped by each other's apartments looking for someone to play with. One particular time, Dorothy entered the door of the Barretts' railway flat, where each room opened to the next in a straight line. Rushing through the kitchen and living room, she ran right into Mrs. Barrett's bedroom. To her surprise, Mrs. Barrett was kneeling by the bed, a rosary in her hands.

Dorothy was so startled she couldn't think of anything to say. But she sensed an inexplicable feeling of warmth toward this devout woman who was not embarrassed to be caught praying. Dorothy never forgot this scene and mentioned it in many articles, as well as in her autobiography.

At last remembering her manners, she stuttered, "Oh! Mrs. Barrett, I'm so sorry to bother you. I'm looking for Kathryn. Is she here?"

Still on her knees, Mrs. Barrett explained, "Kathryn has gone to the store on an errand." Fingering her beads, the woman continued her prayers. Later, Dorothy asked Mrs. Barrett about her religion. The Catholic woman taught her to say the rosary. Dorothy began kneeling by her own bed at night, repeating the prayers she had recently learned.

Her younger sister, Della, was not impressed. The two girls shared a double bed. After an interminable wait, Della would whisper, "Dorothy, come to bed! You must be freezing on the floor." But with her scrawny knees aching, and her body shaking with the cold, Dorothy continued her prayers to the last bead.

"Why don't you join me?" she suggested to Della from time to time. Finally Della did. The two girls began practicing their version of being devout. In their deprived condition in the Chicago slum, religion brought them solace.

But the year Dorothy turned twelve, the family situation improved. John Day landed a position with a substantial salary as sports editor on a Chicago newspaper and moved his family to a spacious home near Lincoln Park. Here in its warmth and comfort Dorothy found safety and peace. The family transferred its membership to the closer Our Saviour Episcopal Church, where Dorothy was finally baptized and prepared for Confirmation. Grace Day noticed a greater interest in religion growing in her older daughter.

The year Dorothy turned fourteen, her mother had a baby boy they named John. After giving birth, Grace Day fell ill and depressed, often unable to care for her new infant. That responsibility fell upon Dorothy. She fixed his bottles, got up in the night when he cried, rocked him to sleep, and pushed him in his baby carriage. She almost came to think of Baby John as her own, loving him as a mother. As he grew, she took him for strolls in his carriage, sometimes leaving their middle-class neighborhood to walk through the grime and misery of the slums the Days had left. Dorothy became aware of the Socialist movement and began reading books by Upton Sinclair and Russian revolutionaries. Her heart went out to Chicago's poor.

One day she passed a young man who caught her eye. He returned the look and seemed equally interested. The young man, Armin Hand, lived next door to Kathryn. He led a band that performed every Sunday in the bandshell in nearby Lincoln Park.

Dorothy and Della attended all of his concerts, including those on Wednesday evenings. Dorothy began to feel an attraction toward Armin, taking every opportunity to see him. She was happy, but not in the right way. The feeling was merely a thrill and didn't provide her with the spiritual happiness she truly craved. When she at last discovered that Armin was married and the father of two children, she realized it was time to forget him and move on to other interests. School was one of them.

Dorothy was an excellent student, and even though she was a year younger than her classmates, she outdid them in English and Latin. She even added private lessons in Greek to her heavy schedule. Her obvious language abilities and talent in writing would eventually earn her a college scholarship. It would come just in time, for her father's newspaper folded. Once again John Day was out of a job.

Dorothy had seen what unemployment and poverty did to families. She watched her young mother's hair turn gray from overwork—washing the laundry by hand in the basement, sewing the girls' dresses and the boys' shirts, searching for materials in bargain sales. Even worse was the stress of turning away bill collectors when there was no money to pay them.

John Day tried to keep up appearances as well as his spirit. When unable to provide his five children with adequate food or a respectable address, he gave them classic books and fine music. He saw learning and culture as far more important than "things." He forbade the children to read dime novels or romances or to listen to the radio. However, he did let them go to the movies where they could see other places and times and visualize the great world outside their neighborhood.

But he was a cold man who never kissed or hugged his children. He avoided them as much as possible, preferring to read and smoke in his easy chair in silence. On the other hand, Grace provided the children with affection and security. She had few interests outside the home and was always present to offer them food, comfort, or a listening ear. She came from a long line of educated people who lived graciously. She did everything possible to do the same with the little her married life provided. She even dressed for dinner, presiding over a laid-out table as though she were a titled lady, not penniless in a tenement.

In 1914, Dorothy graduated with honors from Waller High School, winning a scholarship to college. Only sixteen, she was ready to step out into the world. She chose the University of Illinois at Urbana, far from her controlling parents. On a brisk fall day, she boarded a train for the two-hour ride to the Urbana campus. Filled with hundreds of excited college students, the train left the Chicago station carrying Dorothy to a new life of freedom.

CHAPTER TWO

UNIVERSITY LIFE BRINGS CHANGE

Dorothy's scholarship totaled $300 per year. After paying for registration fees, tuition, and books, she didn't have much left to live on. She was told about a professor with several children who needed help in exchange for room and board. Lonely and missing her two-year-old brother, she gladly took the job.

For her first college term, Dorothy signed up for English Literature, Biology, European History, and Latin, but the only course she enjoyed was English Literature, in which she quickly exhibited an unusual writing talent. She began to write for the school newspaper as well as the local one. Never having taken any interest in sports, she skipped any such requirements. No one seemed to notice. Neither did her fellow students notice the plain, simply dressed younger girl. Dorothy was not invited to join a sorority, and no boys asked her out on dates.

The professor and family with whom she lived were deeply devout Methodists. Dorothy admired their simple, happy faith. But in her heart she wondered why religious people never noticed the poor around them. They heard and read that Jesus admonished his followers to feed the poor, shelter the homeless, and visit the sick. Yet Christians as a whole, it seemed, made no effort to relieve the sufferings of the needy. She wondered, "Why are they all such hypocrites?" And she puzzled over what was wrong.

Ultimately her childhood experiences of God grew dim, and their memory and influence disappeared. She began to scoff at religion, taking God's name in vain for the shock effect, enjoying the look on people's faces when she cursed out loud. Like Karl Marx, Dorothy termed religion "the opiate of the people." She would have none of it.

Several times she ran out of money. She found another room in the home of a teacher and paid for it by doing the washing and ironing. The house was bare and cold, and the job didn't include meals. One time she had nothing to eat for three days. Listless from hunger, she lay in bed, bundled under the covers, and read. Reading had always been her favorite occupation. She took odd jobs to buy more books and sometimes was lucky enough to sell an article to a newspaper.

Dorothy didn't care much for college or for her courses. In later years she wrote that she learned more from books she read on her own than from any class she had taken.

One thing she did learn at college was social activism. She had only been at the university one term when she was invited to a meeting of the Socialists on campus. A new friend, Marie Oberlander, took her along. Here were young people like herself who had dropped the religions of their childhood, shocked at rich America's indifference to the poor. Most were willing to go to jail for causes they considered unjust.

Members of this group were not like most students on campus—rich, spoiled, young people who dressed in name-brand clothes and looked down on Jews and other "undesirables," keeping them out of their clubs and sororities. At last Dorothy had found a group that accepted her. Everything these young Socialists did appealed to her, and she was more than willing to join in their efforts.

On the train to Urbana, Dorothy had noticed an attractive female student with curly red hair, but she then forgot her as college started. But at a Socialist rally she finally met the girl with the striking red hair. Her name was Rayna Simons and the two immediately discovered many interests in common: Russian literature, classical music, and poetry.

Dorothy had never met anyone with an interest in politics before. In her sheltered home she had known few people of any political party. Her father, always a loner, rarely invited anyone over; her shy mother never entertained neighbors. Their lives centered on the dining room table, books, and family.

Rayna was slightly built, Jewish, and wealthy. Although the daughter of a member of Chicago's Board of Trade, she lived in a boarding house. She invited Dorothy to be her roommate, which ended the poorer student's worries.

Rayna's father owned a large farm with horses. On weekends the two girls would drive to the farm to enjoy the fresh country air and ride through the fields, their long hair streaming behind them. Some of their friends complained that Dorothy was taking advantage of Rayna, but Rayna enjoyed her companionship and acceptance. The redhead was three years older, a senior, and engaged to Samson Raphaelson, a Jewish boy who also attended the University of Illinois. The threesome went everywhere together. However, Samson became increasingly jealous of Dorothy's continued friendship with the girl he loved.

Dorothy had no intention of breaking up her friendship with Rayna. No longer alone and depressed, she enjoyed and relished every hour with the handsome, fun-loving couple. The threesome went together to plays, concerts, picnics, and lectures. Rayna was interested in everything Dorothy did or suggested. And whatever Rayna did, she entered into it with her whole heart.

Rayna admired the younger girl's talent. She and Samson both worked on the university paper, as did most of their friends. Everything Dorothy submitted was accepted. But the paper was more than an outlet for her writing. She loved both Rayna and Samson for themselves, knowing that friendships such as theirs came only rarely in a lifetime.

But this friendship was soon to end, as were her college days at Urbana. In 1916, at the close of her sophomore year, her father was offered an important position at the *Morning Telegraph* in New York City. He left Chicago that spring to start work as the sports editor, and once school was out, the rest of the Day family followed.

While at the university, Dorothy had considered herself an independent adult, totally free of her family. But the thought of hundreds of miles between her and her baby brother, John, and sister, Della, seemed too great a separation. Dorothy withdrew from college to follow her family to New York, thus ending her formal education.

The Day family rented a large apartment on New York's West Side, and Dorothy began looking for a newspaper job. She already had experience as a journalist, having written book reviews for the *Chicago Examiner,* in addition to working on the university paper. But John Day quickly made it plain that he thought women belonged at home, and most certainly not in the tough, smoke-filled rooms of a big city paper. He may even have phoned several newspaper friends, telling them not to hire her, because after pounding the pavement for several weeks, she had still not landed a job. She found living at home increasingly difficult as her father treated her like a child. Dorothy had experienced two years of independence at college and was desperate to find work so she could move out of the stifling atmosphere at home. Her chance finally arrived.

The Call was a Socialist newspaper on the lower East Side. Dorothy had picked up several copies and thought, "Maybe they can use a woman journalist to write from the female point of view."

One hot day in August 1916, she dropped by *The Call's* small, grimy office in one of Manhattan's dreariest slums. She asked to speak to the editor. The paper was upstairs over a printing business on Cherry Street. An elevated train clattered by only a few feet from the filthy windows of the one large room where men were busy at work putting out *The Call's* next edition.

The editor turned out to be a short, blond man named Chester White. He looked at the nicely dressed eighteen-year-old girl in hat, gloves, and stockings and wondered what she wanted.

Dorothy explained, "I'm looking for a job here. I've worked on several papers in and around Chicago. Would you care to see some of my writing?" She drew several articles from her portfolio.

"Just a minute, young lady," said the editor, putting out an ink-stained hand to stop her. "We don't need anyone here. Besides, I can't pay you, there's no extra money."

Dorothy didn't give up easily. She had read in other papers about a contest to see how small a salary working girls could live on. "I bet I can live on only five dollars a week," she declared. "I could write about how I did it. Lots of waitresses and factory girls get by on less."

"Five dollars a week?" laughed Mr. White. "Impossible! But if you can do it for a month, why, I'll hire you. I'll even give you a raise to twelve dollars!"

Dorothy's heart skipped a beat. She had a chance at a job and on a Socialist paper. But how would she break the news to her conservative father? She rushed home to tell her mother and began packing her things. All of them fit into one brown suitcase.

She was packed and gone before John Day arrived home from work. Her distraught mother was left to break the shocking news to the furious man.

Dorothy carried the heavy suitcase to the office, leaving it there while she searched for a room to rent. She walked past one miserable tenement after another. From each came stenches forcing her to hold a handkerchief over her nose. Cries and shouts burst from the windows. Shrill pitches came from street vendors along the crowded streets.

Finally she arrived at a nicer building with a sign in the window, "Room to Let." She entered the dark, smelly hallway where toys and garbage were strewn across the unwashed tile floor. Up, up she climbed to the top floor. The room was at the back of an apartment that fronted on the street. The Jewish housewife obviously kept the living room and kitchen clean enough, and she seemed kind and friendly. Dorothy decided to rent the small room whose only window opened on an airshaft. One toilet on the landing served all the occupants of that floor. Washing was done at a sink in the kitchen. But the little bedroom seemed clean and cost only three dollars per week. That left two dollars for food and carfare. The tenement was close enough to her office so she could walk to work. A single burner in her room would do for cooking.

The first night Dorothy hardly slept a wink as bedbugs crawled over her and bit every part of her body. When the winter arrived, she suffered from the cold. The only heat was from the gas burner on which she cooked. Shivering, she often thought longingly of her parents' comfortable apartment and wholesome food.

Her newspaper series was headlined, "How *New York Call*'s Diet Squad Tries Life on $5 per Week." With her first byline, Dorothy had proved it could be done. She was hired fulltime at *The Call* and received the promised raise to $12.00.

Her job was to cover union meetings and strikes, as well as the city's many tragedies, such as children dying in tenement fires, police attacks on picket lines, and protests against the war (World War I). Her hours were midday to midnight. This required walking alone through the dark streets of the dangerous lower East Side. Sometimes friendly cops escorted her home.

After three months with the cold and bedbugs, she was ready to move. One day walking along the East River, she passed a small Episcopal church. In the window of the parish house was a sign, "Rooms to Let." Certainly this would have to be better than the house on Cherry Street. The rector's wife showed Dorothy around. The available room was unheated, but appeared clean. The young journalist moved in, the first of many changes of address.

By 1917 the war in Europe had been raging for three years. The United States finally entered on the side of the Allies. Socialists opposed sending America's young men to fight across the seas. There were many protests, particularly among college students who faced the draft. That April, Dorothy was given the newspaper assignment to accompany a group of Columbia University students to Washington, D.C., to protest the passage of the Conscription Act. She rode with the students on a bus to Washington to cover the event. This was more than an assignment; it was a great adventure. It was Dorothy's first trip on a bus, the first time to see her nation's capital.

En route to the capital, the group stopped for rallies at other campuses. In Philadelphia there was a fight between conservative, patriotic students and the radicals from Columbia. Several men were injured, others arrested and carried off to jail. She had her first glimpse of the mob spirit and found the feeling of brutality that

swept through a mob to be a mysterious thing. Later, she would see much bloodier riots where mounted police deliberately rode down strikers, beating unarmed men into bloody pulp.

With America finally at war, unemployment ended, and most men had jobs to support their families. However, the cost of living rose along with prosperity. There were bread riots and even bombings by anarchists. Dorothy wasn't certain where she stood: was she a Socialist, a Communist, an anarchist? She felt drawn to the farthest left and ultimately joined the International Workers of the World, a radical labor organization.

One time she was assigned to cover Leon Trotsky, a Bolshevik leader who had come to New York to rally people to support the Communist Revolution in Russia. After being exiled to Siberia, he had been thrown out of Russia, France, Germany, and Italy. At that time he was working in Manhattan on a Russian-language Socialist newspaper. Not long afterwards, Russia's Czarist regime was overthrown, and Trotsky returned to that country under its new name of the U.S.S.R. (the Union of Soviet Socialist Republics).

Just two months later, Dorothy covered a hysterical rally in Madison Square Garden where thousands celebrated the overthrow of the Romanov czars. The crowd shouted and sang and waved the country's new red flag with its hammer and sickle. She was moved by the rally's enthusiasm for the new regime that had changed the lives of one-sixth of humanity. But instead of prosperity and security, the Communist Revolution ultimately brought hunger and death.

Another subject of great general interest at that time was birth control. Most clergy were against it, citing scripture and the duty of women to procreate. Those in favor of birth control said it would free women from constant childbearing to do other things; even better, it would relieve overpopulation and its resulting poverty.

Dorothy was sent to cover meetings of the Birth Control League and to cover a clinic opened by Margaret Sanger in Brooklyn. Sanger was the leader of the Birth Control movement and was often jailed for her work. Her sister, Ethel Byrne, a nurse, ran the clinic. To get her story, Dorothy hung around the clinic every day. One afternoon police raided the clinic, and Ethel was taken to prison on Blackwell's Island. There she went on a hunger strike.

Rumors came from the prison that Ethel Byrne was being force-fed, was being brutalized by the prison guards, and was close to death. Afraid of the political consequences if she should die, the governor released the woman.

Dorothy had a true journalist's urge to get at the truth. She followed Ethel Byrne home to her apartment on Manhattan's West Side and stopped her at the door to get her story. Prison and the guards had not harmed Mrs. Byrne. Neither had her fast. Actually, the woman looked quite well. But newspapers expected journalists to report on the darker side of life. Dorothy had to phone in quite a different story, something she always regretted following her conversion.

Working in an office full of men, Dorothy was bound to find romance there. Also, she suffered from great loneliness. Alienated from her father, she was not welcome at home. John Day felt humiliated by his elder daughter's work at a Socialist newspaper and by the stories she wrote for it. Sometimes Grace Day and Della sneaked in a visit or lunch with Dorothy. But they felt out of place in that poor section of the city where Dorothy worked and lived. With seven million people all around her, Dorothy felt completely alone. She was only nineteen.

Lifting her from despair was Mike Gold, a twenty-five-year-old journalist. He would eventually become the editor of the Communist paper *The Daily Worker*. But at this point in Dorothy's life, Mike was city editor of *The Call*. He and its other young writers sometimes joined her for dinner at a nearby Child's Restaurant, then afterwards smoked and talked for hours.

Mike was born and raised in New York. He read and admired much of the same Russian literature Dorothy found so compelling. It was Mike who accompanied her to Madison Square Garden to cover the huge rally celebrating the Russian Revolution. He also helped her when she was in need.

Dorothy came down with the flu and was unable to crawl out of bed to shop, get medicine, or even eat. She hadn't shown up at the newspaper office or even called in for days. Mike phoned her, saying, "I'm really worried about you. I'll try to come by after work and bring you something to eat." As it turned out, he had to work past midnight and did not arrive until after one. He brought her supper and cough medicine, and they ate together in her tiny room. He stayed to help her until 6:30 A.M.

The rector's wife was shocked to find Dorothy had allowed a man to stay in her room overnight. She phoned Dorothy's mother, who was equally upset. Grace Day rushed down to the rectory to check on her daughter's condition. She was not nearly as upset over her daughter's chastity as she was over her health. When she found Dorothy in the bare, cold room, Grace insisted her daughter move out.

Mike and others at the office had long ago recommended that Dorothy try a better neighborhood around Greenwich Village where most of them lived. As soon as Dorothy was up to it, Grace helped her move to a new location on Eighth Street. The area had many small family-run restaurants where writers at *The Call* had coffee or ate supper together. In the same vicinity was a larger establishment, Webster Hall, which held dances and parties that attracted the bohemian artists and writers who lived in Greenwich Village.

A young anarchist who often ate there took a liking to Dorothy. One night at an anti-conscription meeting, he rushed over, calling and waving to her as he crossed the dance floor. Reaching her, he grabbed her and tried to give her a kiss. Without thinking, Dorothy slapped him hard across the mouth. He returned the slap, which she followed up with a solid shove. The frail young man fell to the floor. Two reporters attending the same event wrote up the incident in their papers. The next morning their stories appeared in the *New York Times* and the *World*.

Arriving at work, Dorothy saw everyone reading the story about her. She realized that she had embarrassed the paper and resigned. She spent the next four days looking for a new job and found one at the Anti-Conscription League at fifteen dollars a week. There she had regular work hours with no late-night assignments. Her parents were pleased at the change, and Dorothy would have stayed on except for a chance encounter.

CHAPTER THREE

STARTING OVER

While covering assignments and attending meetings, Dorothy often came across Charles Wood, drama critic of the *Masses,* a leftist magazine frequently under suspicion. One day walking crosstown on 14th Street, Dorothy ran into Wood. Doffing his hat, he stopped and said, "I haven't seen you around lately. What are you up to these days?"

The young journalist explained that she was no longer with *The Call.* "Right now I'm helping out at the Anti-Conscription League, doing general office work," she shrugged. "It's just temporary."

Charles replied, "I'm on my way to lunch with my editor, Floyd Dell. Can you join us? It's not far. Just across Third Avenue."

Dorothy smiled, "Why not? Sounds fine to me."

At the small bistro, following an introduction and some small talk, Dorothy felt enough at ease with the tall, thin editor to blurt out, "Why not let me write a review for your magazine? Right now I have plenty of time."

Dell liked the idea. Later, after reading Dorothy's excellent review of a new play, he hired her as the magazine's assistant editor. This was a great achievement for an aspiring young writer. Many contributors to the

Masses were already well known, some destined to become famous.

The *Masses* was on the fourth floor of a building overlooking Union Square, a part of New York City associated with union protests and Communist rallies.

Dorothy started her job April 23, 1917, perhaps the youngest assistant editor in the city. And in fact, her first three days there she acted as editor, because Dell had to go out of town. Her job was to go through the stacks of mail (most of it articles submitted by hopeful writers) and select stories and essays for the magazine's next issue. Europe was in the throes of World War I, with America about to send its young men across the Atlantic to the deadly battlefields. But most contributors to the *Masses* were pacifists concerned with overturning the political scene at home. They wrote about Communism and sexual freedom to shock their conservative elders.

Dorothy had only been with the publication a week when Dell invited her to move in with him and two other male staff writers. Their apartment was on Mac-Dougal Street in Greenwich Village above an experimental theater called the Provincetown Playhouse. The three men planned to be there only until June, after which each would go off to vacation in the mountains or the seashore. Dorothy would have the place to herself all summer. She was delighted.

After moving in, she entertained her Socialist friends, talking all night about literature, the Russian Revolution, and avoiding the draft. She also made friends with many of the playwrights and actors of the Provincetown Playhouse, spending evenings with them at the Golden Swan, a nearby restaurant. Many of these people would later become famous. One was Eugene O'Neill, with whom she fell in love. O'Neill would be America's only playwright to win the Nobel Prize and authored such works as *A Moon for the Misbegotten* and *Long Day's Journey into Night*.

An already well-known person who frequented the place was journalist John Reed. In 1920 Reed would die in Russia of hunger and disease. But in 1917, sitting at the tables of the Golden Swan, he was a healthy, talented young man filled with enthusiasm for Communism. Although he had published several books, his most famous was yet to be written: *Ten Days That Shook the World*, his eyewitness account of the Russian Revolution. Decades later, this best-selling book would be made into the feature film *Reds*.

In 1917 America entered the war. Thousands of young men were conscripted and sent overseas. Dorothy and her circle were adamantly opposed to the war. Most were pacifists, and many were arrested for refusing to register for the draft or for refusing to serve when called up. Many of the young men were treated terribly in jail; one even died in custody. All were denied their civil rights.

The country regarded Marxists and other supporters of the Russian Revolution as enemies of the state. Because the *Masses* supported anarchists and Communists, the magazine was considered too dangerous to publish during wartime. Its mailing permit was canceled, and the owners were put on trial for sedition. The final issue of the *Masses* was printed in December. Once again Dorothy was out of work. Some of the staff moved to Chicago and started a similar magazine they named the *Liberator*. Dorothy would join them later.

She was also still seeing Mike Gold, the two taking long walks together along New York's East River, sometimes sitting on a pier to watch the shrilling seagulls and the tugboats fighting the strong current. One November evening, the young couple was having supper in a basement restaurant when Peggy Baird came over to talk to them. Peggy was a suffragist. She explained that she was leaving the next day for Washington to picket the White House.

"Come along, Dorothy," she said. "It should be exciting."

Taken by surprise, Dorothy thought a while. Young men were fighting overseas or protesting the draft. Here was something young women could do. She felt women had as much right to vote as men, and she greatly admired the suffragettes who marched up Fifth Avenue, flags and banners flying for their cause. President Woodrow Wilson was not only against giving women the vote, he had led the United States into a distant war. Why not picket the White House and show her dissent? Dorothy agreed to go.

On November 10, she and Peggy boarded the train to Washington. The protesters were arrested, Dorothy along with them. It was the first of her many experiences of jail. There she underwent a ten-day fast protesting America's unjust treatment of political prisoners. Most of the other suffragettes were college-educated women from well-to-do families. Because some socialites were involved in the march as well, the event received tremendous publicity. The women were at last released on November 28.

On her return to New York, Dorothy visited her mother and Della to tell them about the unpleasant events. She saw her family only when her disapproving father was out of town. He was embarrassed by his left-wing daughter. At least he could take pride in his older sons, Donald and Sam, who had enlisted in the U.S. Navy. He certainly did not approve of Dorothy's life in Greenwich Village. She was always changing rooms, changing jobs, changing boyfriends. Meanwhile her social life continued to revolve around the Golden Swan on 4th Street. The pitiful rooms she rented were usually unheated, and at least she could keep warm in the restaurant.

One night at the Golden Swan, Gene O'Neill was getting drunker by the minute. Suddenly, at the table full of writers and actors in the smoke-filled room, he did something that caught at Dorothy's heart and made her rethink the life she was living. He began to recite from memory the very long, beautiful poem "The Hound of Heaven" by Francis Thompson. The poem tells of a soul's continual avoidance of God, even as God gently, relentlessly pursues the soul with love:

I fled Him, down the nights and down the days;
I fled Him, down the arches of the years;
I fled Him, down the Labyrinthine ways
of my own mind; and in the mists of tears
I hid from Him, and under running laughter
up visited hopes, I sped....

Even drunk, O'Neill put so much artistry into his rendition of the poem that it moved Dorothy's soul as nothing had before. She knew then that the "hound of heaven" (a metaphor for God) was at her heels, soon to chase her down. The poem awakened something in her soul that had been dead for years. She started dropping into nearby St. Joseph's Church just to sit and gaze at the altar, her heart lifted to God. Soon she began attending Sunday Mass, then Masses during the week. She read such classic works of spirituality as *The Imitation of Christ* and the *Confessions of St. Augustine.* But she kept this great change a secret from her worldly Socialist friends. They would have laughed at the folly of it, a woman who wrote for Communist newspapers sneaking into Catholic churches to pray!

Dorothy started having second thoughts about her late nights in Greenwich Village and her flirtations with writers and actors. While America's young men were giving their lives in Europe, she should be doing something useful. Many nurses had enlisted to serve overseas; New York hospitals were in dire need of help.

The young journalist turned to a new profession. She applied to King's County Hospital in Brooklyn to enter nurses' training. Her sister, Della, by then eighteen, also registered for the course, which began in January 1918.

Mrs. Day supplied the money for her daughters' outfits, six pink uniforms and twelve white aprons each. Besides attending classes at the hospital, the girls changed sheets, carried bedpans, and gave comfort to a roomful of elderly women with hip fractures. They worked a twelve-hour day, then returned to their rooms to study.

Dorothy began reading the Bible again, adding the lives of the saints and great spiritual works. She attended Sunday Mass with a Catholic nurse in the chapel on the hospital grounds.

Not yet twenty-one, Dorothy was a beautiful young woman, tall, slender, and graceful. The pink uniform added a becoming glow to her fine features. It was no wonder that an orderly, Lionel Moise, took a fancy to her. After her many flings, this time Dorothy knew it was true love.

Lionel Moise was not the usual orderly. He too had been a journalist, in fact, the highest paid at several big-city papers. But ripe for adventure, he had signed on as cameraman for a film being made in Venezuela. On his return trip, he'd been robbed and badly beaten by the crew. Once the ship docked in New York, the crew threw his bloodied body under the elevated train station near King's County Hospital. His body was discovered and taken to the hospital in an ambulance. Following his recovery, he remained there as he had no money and nowhere else to go.

To cover his huge hospital bill, he had offered to work there as an orderly, living for free at the hospital. Nursing students also lived in a wing of the hospital. One day Dorothy and Lionel met in the kitchen. With his broken nose and other injuries, he might not have appealed to most women. Yet after a few dates, Dorothy was ready to give up everything for him.

Eventually, Lionel got some money together and rented an apartment on 35th Street. Unable to think of anyone or anything else, even her patients, Dorothy left King's County Hospital and moved in with him.

He turned out to be wildly jealous and erratic, yet somehow that made her love him even more. Then one day she discovered she was pregnant. Lionel had made it clear from the start that he would not marry her, so her news led to days of arguments and pressure. Finally she agreed to have an illegal abortion. While she was having the procedure, he packed his things, left her forty dollars, and moved out. She returned to the empty apartment to find a note saying he was going to Chicago and that she should find someone rich and marry him. For the rest of her life, Dorothy regretted what she had given up for him.

CHAPTER FOUR

A NEW HOME, A NEW LIFE

After Lionel left, Dorothy seemingly followed his advice. She met a wealthy man—Berkeley Tobey—and, without really caring for him, married him and left for Europe on an extended honeymoon. First they visited England and France. Finally they toured Italy, which Dorothy loved. Six months were spent in beautiful Capri where she wrote her first novel, *The Eleventh Virgin,* based on her own youthful experiences. But in her heart, Dorothy still yearned for Lionel. With only one year of marriage behind her, she divorced Tobey and moved to Chicago. There Lionel worked with several of her old friends from the *Masses* who had started another Communist paper called the *Liberator.*

While in Chicago, Dorothy suffered a humiliation that forever left its impression on her. She had joined the radical labor organization, International Workers of the World. It had a run-down office on Chicago's skid row, with living quarters above the office. A new friend of Dorothy's, Mae Cramer, was also in love with Lionel. When he rejected her, Mae attempted suicide. Once out of the hospital, she called Dorothy, asking for a place to stay. Dorothy suggested the two rooms above the

International Workers of the World office, and Mae shortly moved in.

One night in July 1922, Dorothy received a phone call from Mae begging her for help, as she was too ill to care for herself. Dorothy rushed over to spend the night with her. Around midnight a police group called the "Red Squad" raided the place. Four men burst into their room, accused them of running a house of prostitution, and arrested them. Still in their nightclothes, Dorothy and Mae were herded into a van and taken to the police station. There they were booked as streetwalkers. Mae took it as a joke, having had the experience before. But Dorothy was devastated. This was nothing like being jailed in Washington for a good cause. Here she was body-searched and treated like a prostitute. Her family would die of shame if they knew.

There were six prostitutes crowded into their cell. To keep their dresses clean for court appearances, the women spent the day in their slips. They regarded their time in jail as a vacation, where they received free food and lodging. However, one woman, a drug addict, screamed day and night, beating her head against the cell bars and howling like a banshee. Dorothy thought that no woman in childbirth, or any cancer patient, suffered like that.

Those pitiful drug addicts and streetwalkers could not escape from their profession. They had no education and no skills. But Dorothy knew *her* friends would arrive to bail her out. People of privilege could escape, while these poor women were condemned to their ugly careers. The episode impressed her deeply.

After her release, Dorothy got a job as a court reporter for the City News Bureau. She rented a room with three Catholic women her own age. In viewing their lives, their regular attendance at Mass, and their discreet handling of love affairs without falling into sin, Dorothy began to feel that Catholicism was something rich and real, even fascinating. She was drawn to the church of America's immigrants and underprivileged.

Not long afterwards, she moved to New Orleans with her friend Mary Gordon. They found a place to live in the exotic French Quarter and Dorothy got a job with the *New Orleans Item*. She was assigned to cover "taxi dancers," women who were hired to dance with one man after another for pay. To put reality into her story, one night Dorothy worked as a taxi dancer herself. Her plan backfired when she was assaulted by the other dancers and received a black eye!

But New Orleans had something beautiful to offer. Just down the street from her apartment stood historic St. Louis Cathedral. She often dropped in to pray there and sometimes attended Benediction after work.

One day Mary, an avowed Communist, presented Dorothy with a rosary. Dorothy kept it with her throughout her life and, after her conversion, used it daily.

The year 1924 brought Dorothy the thrill every writer dreams of—her book, *The Eleventh Virgin,* was published. The reviews were embarrassing, it didn't meet with success, and it never sold beyond the first printing, but her agent sold the movie rights for $5,000, half of which was hers. In 1924, $2,500 was a small fortune. No longer needing to work, Dorothy moved back to New York.

This was the first large sum she had ever owned. Now she could go anywhere, do whatever she pleased. What she wanted most was to write. Her old friend, Peggy Baird, suggested, "Don't fritter your money away. Invest it in something worthwhile, like real estate." The seashore had always appealed to the city-bred Dorothy. She took the ferry to Staten Island, and before the day was over she became the owner of a small simple cottage set on a tiny piece of property, right on the beach.

At the age of twenty-six, Dorothy began a totally new life. With a few sticks of furniture, her books, and a typewriter, she moved into the cottage. Free to write whatever she wanted, she turned out essays, stories, and poems, and began working on another book. It was all she had ever dreamed of. She walked on the beach in the early morning, picking up shells, finding driftwood for her cast-iron stove, listening to the piercing cries of terns and seagulls. From her cottage doorway, she could watch great ocean liners majestically cross New York harbor into the open Atlantic. There were fishermen and clammers, and at night the twin lighthouses at Sandy Hook in New Jersey flashed across the sky.

At last Dorothy was at peace, except for the "Hound of Heaven" barking at her heels crying, "Come home. Come home…I'm waiting."

Sometimes she took the ferry back to the city. One evening at a cocktail party at Peggy Baird's apartment, she met Forster Batterham, a biologist and nature lover, as well as an atheist and anarchist. Although they didn't seem to have much in common, Dorothy and Forster dated for a year. Then they decided to live together. Forster didn't believe in laws or in marriage. He wanted to live freely in whatever manner he pleased. He enjoyed camping, mountain climbing, just anything outdoors, but what he loved most was fishing. This he could do at Dorothy's beachfront house on Staten Island. Dorothy lived in the cottage and wrote, while Forster continued his job in the city and came to Staten Island on weekends.

All week Dorothy sat at her typewriter, pounding out articles and chapters of her new book, while awaiting Forster's return on the weekend. Then they would go out in his wooden skiff and fish or dig in the sand for clams for dinner. Forster loved this quiet life and he brought a calming influence into her days. The two enjoyed long walks on the beach. He read the *New York Times* to her over breakfast. They sat quietly on a derelict pier, dangling fishing lines in the waves. At times he shared his knowledge of marine life, explaining about the sea creatures around them on the beach and in the waters.

Each evening an Angelus bell pealed at nearby St. Joseph's Catholic Church. On hearing it Dorothy would stop to thank God for her beautiful new surroundings, the sparkling sea lapping at the shore, the peace and quiet of her new simple life.

CHAPTER FIVE

TAMAR

The 1920s are known as the Flapper Age. Dorothy was very much a part of it. She cropped her long brown hair, smoked, and when in Manhattan danced the Charleston and drank at cocktail parties.

Dorothy loved Forster, but *his* feelings for her were nowhere near as hungry and desperate. One thing she yearned for was a baby. For years she had been afraid that her earlier abortion had destroyed any chance of having a child. Still her longing for motherhood grew within her. Then one day, in the summer of 1925, Dorothy suspected she might be pregnant again. A month later she was certain. Had God forgiven her for her earlier sin? Her heart overflowed with joy and thankfulness.

Forster did not share her happiness. He had no desire to take on the care and trouble of a child who would surely disturb their tranquil life.

Dorothy began to pray. Searching the cottage, she found the rosary given her by Mary Gordon in New Orleans years ago. Each day, as she walked to the post office in the nearby village of Huguenot, she recited the prayers, holding the blue beads in her hand. Was she saying the prayers correctly? It didn't really matter. Just praying made her happy.

On her way to the post office stood the little chapel of St. Joseph. It was nothing like the huge, ornate Catholic churches in New York and Europe. It was small, warm, and inviting. Dorothy began stopping in for daily visits, just sitting quietly before the sacrament in reserve. Feeling a bit strange and out of place, she was embarrassed to ask anyone, particularly a priest, about prayer or religion. After all, she was living with a man, and everyone in the small town knew they weren't married.

One day as she was on her way to the post office, a nun bumped into her. Blushing and embarrassed, the nun introduced herself as Sister Aloysia. Here was the opening Dorothy needed to ask questions about the Catholic Church.

"Good morning, Sister," she said, "I'm Dorothy Day. I live at the little cottage on the dune over there." She pointed seaward.

From the blackness of her habit, Sister Aloysia withdrew her pale white hand and offered it. "Have you been in our little chapel yet?" she inquired. "It's a gem."

Dorothy blushed, ashamed she had been there but never spoken to anyone. "Yes, I have," she replied, not commenting further.

"Well, I'm heading that way. Come with me," invited the Sister.

The two women walked along the trail to the simple wooden church. Inside Sister Aloysia led Dorothy past the sanctuary and outside into the sunlight. The area behind the church was filled with activity. An old man was shucking clams, two women were peeling vegetables, and another stirred the contents of a giant pot.

"This is our soup kitchen," announced Sister Aloysia proudly. "It's all volunteer. Perhaps you'd like to help."

"Not today. Maybe some other time," replied Dorothy. "But who eats at your soup kitchen? Isn't this a resort area?"

"Many homeless families live among the dunes. Some have been evicted from apartments in the city; others are illegal immigrants hiding from the authorities. We don't ask questions; we just help."

Dorothy had written about the poor and needy. Here was a chance to help them directly. She returned to peel and cook when Forster was in the city.

One day Sister Aloysia dropped by Dorothy's cottage and invited her to attend Mass at St. Joseph's.

Dorothy looked down at her hands. "I can't say for sure. Forster will be here for the weekend. He's against religion. He might not like having me go." But she went anyway, that Sunday and regularly afterwards.

Each time Forster watched her getting dressed up, he asked, "Where to? Church again?" He was jealous of anything that took Dorothy away from his side. That it was organized religion, something he thoroughly detested, made him even angrier. Religion became a wall between them.

Summer passed in writing, reading, walking on the beach, and praying. By September she knew for certain she was pregnant. This was surely a miracle; doctors in New York had warned her she might never conceive again. By December her condition was plainly visible, and she saw it as a clear sign that God had forgiven her.

The very thought of the new life within her filled her with joy and thanksgiving.

Peggy Baird had given Dorothy a small statue of the Virgin Mary. Dorothy often glanced toward the blue and gold statue and lifted her heart in praise. She sang the "Te Deum" she had learned by heart long ago at her Episcopal church. At last she was at peace with herself.

One thing she wanted for her child was that it be baptized in the Catholic Church. When she shared her dream with Sister Aloysia, the nun was delighted. "But what about you?" she inquired.

Dorothy shook her head. If she became a Catholic, she would have to give up the help and security of living with Forster. But she wanted to have her child baptized a Catholic, cost what it may. She did not want her daughter or son floundering through youth as she had done, doubting and hesitating, undisciplined and amoral. Dorothy thought that baptism was the greatest thing she could do for her child. For herself, she prayed for the gift of faith. She would need it, because she knew that becoming a Catholic would mean facing life alone.

As the time for her delivery drew close, Dorothy moved into her sister sister's apartment in Manhattan. There she would be near a big modern hospital. Back in the city, she was again able to attend Mass in a church every day. She registered for her delivery at Bellevue Hospital where the clinic and ten-day stay after the birth were free. She went there each week for an examination, delighted that all was going smoothly.

On the second of March she experienced her first labor pains. Her time had come. Della fetched a taxi and the two rushed off to the hospital. Dorothy, bedded in a long ward, suffered all afternoon and throughout the night. At 5:00 A.M. on March 4, 1926, the baby was born—a beautiful little girl. Dorothy named her Tamar Teresa. Tamar means "little palm."

Dorothy was filled with joy and thanks that God had given her a second chance to be a mother. She felt that no human creature could receive or contain so great a flood of love as she felt after the birth of Tamar. Ten days later she and the baby were released from the hospital. After a short stay at Della's, she returned to Staten Island on the ferry, carrying her precious baby in a pink blanket.

Forster was unexpectedly thrilled at becoming a father. He found Tamar a delight, even taking part in her care. But he was adamant that he did not want their baby baptized. He called the ceremony mumbo jumbo, a fuss peculiar to women. Many times when the subject came up, he stamped out of the cottage and returned to Manhattan.

At this time Dorothy's father moved to Florida, where he was one of the founders of the Hialeah Race Track. He asked Dorothy to board her fourteen-year-old brother, John, over the summer at her beachfront cottage.

Dorothy had been having some financial difficulty and was glad for the extra money. Also, she had always loved her younger brother. John arrived and enjoyed the freedom of the seashore, as well as helping with his tiny niece, Tamar.

Only two blocks away on Hylan Boulevard was St. Joseph's Home, a Catholic refuge for unwed mothers. Sister Aloysia worked there, caring for and teaching the younger children. During her free time she walked to Dorothy's cottage to prepare her for the baby's baptism. Sister would first peek in the back window and call out, "Is he there?" referring to Forster, known to all for his antireligious feelings. Once the way was clear, she would sweep into the cottage in her long black habit, loaded down with books for Dorothy's spiritual enlightenment. Three times a week Sister Aloysia taught Dorothy catechism lessons designed for her fourth-grade students. She expected Dorothy to memorize each lesson by the next visit. Dorothy tried her best, but at twenty-nine and with a baby to care for, it was hard to learn anything by heart.

Tamar was baptized in late June at St. Joseph's Chapel. Afterwards a christening party was held at Dorothy's cottage with many of her neighbors attending. Her Socialist friends, most of them Communist Jews, were mystified by the turn of events. Had motherhood made Dorothy lose her senses? They were further stunned when Dorothy herself was baptized soon after, with Sister Aloysia as her godmother!

As a Catholic, Dorothy Day had many shadows in her background: She had had an abortion; she had been married, if only for a year, and divorced; now she was an unwed mother, living with the baby's father. In the interest of baby Tamar, Father Hyland offered a solution: If Dorothy and Forster would get married, perhaps in time the Church would annul her earlier marriage to Berkeley.

Forster would hear none of it. As an anarchist he refused to be part of such a ceremony, one that involved officials of state or church. "I will not be a liar or a hypocrite," he proclaimed.

Throughout the summer, the two tried to come to some understanding for the sake of Tamar. But as Dorothy gave more and more time to the baby and to God, Forster felt he was being squeezed out. Much as he loved little Tamar, that fall Forster took a final leave of Dorothy.

Dorothy couldn't bear to be alone. She closed the beach house with its many memories of love and happiness and moved back to the city.

CHAPTER SIX

PETER MAURIN

Dorothy moved into a rooming house on West 14th Street, placing Tamar in a nursery while at work. She found a job writing one-page descriptions of novels for a publisher, and also worked from ten to three for a radical peace organization called the Fellowship of Reconciliation.

Her rooms were near Our Lady of Guadalupe Church where she was able to attend daily Mass. Her sister, Della, who sometimes babysat for her, had gotten married and was expecting her first child. Dorothy had constant financial worries, especially about the back taxes on her beach cottage. The next season she rented it out to summer visitors and worked for the Marist Fathers' summer camp on Staten Island.

Then came an unexpected break. The Pathé Motion Picture Company read a play Dorothy had written and admired her talent. They offered her a contract at $125 per week to work on movie scripts! The summer of 1929 Dorothy and Tamar left by train for Hollywood.

Dorothy found a place to live and a nursery school for Tamar. But even earning $500 a month, she felt financially stretched. Besides, she didn't enjoy the lifestyle in the movie capital. She was a very social creature who

46

needed community. But it was hard for an Easterner to break into established California groups.

When Dorothy's three-month contract was not renewed, she and Tamar returned to New York. There she wrote articles for *Commonweal, The Oratory,* and other Catholic publications. However, the pay wasn't enough to support two people. Then *Commonweal*'s editor assigned her to write a series of articles on life in Mexico. Though Mexico was a traditionally Catholic country, its government was now persecuting priests and had closed convents and monasteries.

Dorothy bought a Model T Ford and, loading Tamar into the old car, set off for Mexico. She fell in love with the country, its color, and the piety of the people. In her articles she told of the beautiful processions on Palm Sunday and other feasts. But she was shocked by the laws against religious expression of any kind. She would have stayed in Mexico longer, but Tamar came down with malaria. The worried mother took her sick child back to New York for medical treatment.

Over the next few years Dorothy moved around constantly, partly due to poverty, but perhaps as a way to avoid Forster. She spent two summers on Staten Island and winters in Florida at her mother's place in Coconut Grove. While there she wrote articles on Florida's migrant workers for *Commonweal*. The next summer she got a job with the newspaper *CSI Advance* to write a gardening column. She found her information by driving around Staten Island to interview people about their beautiful gardens.

By then Tamar was five. Her life had been one move after another, most recently to a tenement on 12th

Street, then another on 15th Street. The latter had a fenced garden at the rear of the building where she could play while her mother wrote articles, both for Communist and for Catholic magazines.

Dorothy saw many similarities between Communism and Christianity. She believed Christians should live together, sharing everything in common as they did in the first century. The luxury of most bishops horrified her. Why should there be a few very rich people while millions lived in poverty, suffering sickness and early death? But she wondered, "What could one woman do to change it?"

Months passed and her frustrations grew. Jesus had told his followers to feed the poor, shelter the homeless, visit the sick and prisoners, and care for widows and orphans. Yet she was doing none of it.

At that time, November 1932, America was in the depths of the Great Depression, with millions unemployed and starving. Communists and labor unions organized a hunger march on Washington, D.C. Both *Commonweal* and the Jesuit magazine *America* gave Dorothy paid assignments to cover the march.

Several large buses waited at Union Square to carry New York's seven hundred marchers to the nation's capital. No provisions were made for the marchers to eat or sleep, and there were no sanitary facilities on the buses.

Residents of Washington were aware that this caravan of poor, ragged people was about to descend on them. The city was traumatized by the "Red scare." Hordes of police were called out to handle the controversial parade. Many marchers were beaten or trampled by horses. Dorothy was right in the middle of things. During the fight between marchers and police, an officer's club broke two of her ribs. Even so she completed her articles and telegraphed them to her newspapers.

Later that morning she walked to the site where the future shrine of the Immaculate Conception was under construction. Services were held then in the underground crypt. It was December 8, the Feast of the Immaculate Conception, a "holy day of obligation" in her new faith. As a Catholic, it was now her duty to attend Mass on that Marian feast.

Dorothy made her way down the steps to the chapel in the crypt. Kneeling, she wept quietly, begging God to show her the path he wanted her to take. How should she use her life and talents to help the poor? In the hushed silence, broken only by the shuffling feet of worshippers moving forward to receive Communion, she finally found the peace she had sought. Just one day later, she would discover that God had answered her prayer.

The next day Dorothy arrived back in New York City. At that time she and little Tamar shared an apartment on East 15th Street with her younger brother, John, his wife, Tessa, and their baby. Tamar had been left with Tessa while Dorothy was in Washington.

Hearing footsteps on the stairs, Tamar rushed to greet her mother. "Someone's here!" she shouted, pulling Dorothy into the cozy kitchen.

A man Dorothy had never seen before was the center of attention, everyone gathered around him. He was talking and gesturing excitedly.

John introduced them. "Dorothy, this is Peter Maurin. He's been looking all over New York for you."

Dorothy appraised the stranger. Peter Maurin was short and broad-shouldered, with the square, open face of a peasant. His clothes were worn and dirty, and he had obviously not bathed in a long time.

The stranger stood up. He introduced himself in a strong foreign accent then said, "I have come for your help."

Peter Maurin was born in 1877 in Languedoc in Southern France. He was one of twenty-three children of a poor farmer and his wife. Peter left home at fourteen to become a Christian Brother, eventually leaving the order when he was twenty.

In 1909 he sailed for Canada, expecting to homestead. He worked his way around the country as a farmhand. The same love for God that had called him to the Christian Brothers never left the simple farmer. Wherever he went, he preached to anyone nearby about God and the great sacrifice of Jesus on the cross for humanity. But to Peter the modern age had lost the sense of the sacred, and people had become too involved in the acquisition of material things. He felt that the present was no improvement on the past and that radical change was needed.

Hoping to reach more people, in 1911 Peter crossed the border illegally into the United States. His heavy accent made it almost impossible for Americans to understand him; his shabby appearance turned many away. Unaware of the hopelessness of his task, he continued to preach and teach everywhere he went.

One theme he emphasized above all others was the need for Christians to live in community, helping one another physically and spiritually. But he needed a better way to spread his message.

In the course of his travels around New York City, Peter somehow met George Shuster, editor of *Commonweal,* the Catholic magazine Dorothy wrote for. On hearing Peter's vision for Catholics, George recognized many of the same ideas Dorothy had expressed in her articles. George gave Peter her address and suggested he look her up.

Peter had no interest in money or material comforts. He slept anywhere he could. When no hospitality was offered, he was content to spend the night on a park bench. The warmth and fellowship of the Days' kitchen opened his heart. As the two chatted that first night, Peter discovered that Dorothy was a recent convert to the Church. He immediately took it upon himself to be her teacher in the Catholic faith.

The two sat across the kitchen table surveying each other. Pointing a finger at her, Peter told her of his dream for the Catholic Church. In his thick French accent, he began: "The true Christian life as Jesus taught it can be lived by anyone. If enough people follow the gospel, they can change the world! My dream is for believers to live in community, owning everything in common like the first Christians."

Dorothy's blue eyes lit up. Here at last was a Catholic who thought as she did. "Of course," she said, "that's my dream, too."

He struck the kitchen table with his fist. "Then there would be no more hunger, no more wars. Everyone

would love and care for his neighbor, his Christian brother."

"You're so right," chimed in Dorothy. "It sounds exactly like what the Communists teach. But without their harshness and cruelty."

Peter's voice dropped low so she could hardly hear. "There is dynamite in Christ's gospel, but the Church is afraid to try it. What about you?"

"I'm not afraid," she replied. "Let's start now. But how can we reach the people, spread the message?"

Peter had no problem with that. "What we need is a publication, a newspaper to spread the word. You're a writer; I've done some writing myself. What more do we need?"

"Money!" Dorothy said, as everyone broke out in laughter.

Peter said, "We must begin at once to make this dream of Christian community come true."

CHAPTER SEVEN

THE CATHOLIC WORKER

Dorothy had been making her confessions at the Paulist Fathers' church on West 59th Street. After she told Father Joseph McSorley about her desire to start a newspaper, the kindly priest offered to print the first edition of the paper for $57.00.

A big decision was a name for the publication. Because Dorothy was so concerned with the workers of the world, especially the Catholic workers, that was what they named it, *The Catholic Worker.*

With enough material to fill eight pages, she took it to Paulist Press to be printed. As soon as the copies came off the press, Dorothy and three young men went to Union Square to hawk the paper. The price was a penny, but most copies were given away.

The first issue of *The Catholic Worker* was published May 1, 1933. May Day was the biggest day of the year for Socialists, Communists, radicals, and anarchists. They paraded through Union Square by the thousands, carrying flags and banners. Dorothy knew the Union Square event well, as she had worked for the *Masses* there. Besides, she had lived near Union Square off and on for years. This was the perfect day and place to launch her newspaper. In one hour every copy was gone. She was delighted!

Back at the apartment, Dorothy and Peter made plans for a second edition, this time to number 10,000 copies. Peter wrote a long article for it on economics and the agrarian farm movement. He wanted people to leave their crowded, unhealthy cities and live in farm communes where they could provide their own food. Dorothy wrote a column she later called "On Pilgrimage," that appeared in almost every issue for the next forty-seven years.

Readers of *The Catholic Worker* came to help with its production and distribution. Among them were college students, priests, writers, idealists. Soon Dorothy needed more space, so she rented the store on the main floor of the apartment house to use as an office. Then she leased another building next door to house all the workers, as well as the poor who began showing up for food and shelter.

Peter spoke many times about his vision to open houses of hospitality. Soon they were on their way. Dorothy and her helpers prepared huge pots of soup. They bought bags of old bread for pennies. Word spread quickly through the slums that there was food free for the asking. Every morning a long line of unemployed men and homeless families waited outside the building in the cold.

Dorothy begged grocery stores for leftover or damaged potatoes and vegetables. Then she peeled and boiled them for the soup. Soon her hands became rough and red from so much peeling and cutting. But inside she felt warm with happiness for she was obeying Christ's command to "feed my flock."

Meanwhile, her father, John Day, Sr., was moving among America's wealthiest people as part owner of the posh Hialeah Racetrack in Florida. He would gladly have disowned his strange daughter with her Socialist ideas. Why couldn't Dorothy live decently like the rest of the family? Her three brothers were successful in their careers. Sam Houston Day eventually became editor of *The New York Journal-American,* and later young John and his wife would move to Dobbs Ferry, an elite town on the Hudson, where he was also editor of a newspaper. The older brothers and their father avoided contact with Dorothy out of embarrassment. What was wrong with her? The answer was obvious: she had become a Catholic and an advocate for the poor, and preferred living in a slum among the poorest Jews and immigrants in New York.

In the early 1900s, Catholics in America were a group apart, a people within a people. They were not accepted socially and, even when financially successful, were turned down by country clubs and elite prep schools. Catholics had their own societies, each a separate national origin: Irish, German, Italian, Spanish, Polish.

Like Peter Maurin, Dorothy believed that the social order must be changed, and that it was wrong for property to be mainly in the hands of the wealthy few. She thought that a Christian revolution would prevent a social revolution, but in order to do that, the communal aspects of early Christianity had to be restored, and somehow placed in combination with providing some measure of property for all.

For the remainder of their lives, Peter Maurin and Dorothy Day worked to make this dream a reality.

The Catholic Worker grew to a circulation of 150,000 and was soon paying its own way. By renting more buildings around them, Dorothy and Peter were able to provide rooms for the growing numbers of destitute men, women, and families who came to them. The paper brought publicity about their work, while their work increased the circulation.

The Catholic Worker came into the hands of idealistic priests, seminarians, and members of religious orders, but especially Catholic college students. Their hearts were moved by the stories and essays illustrating the tragedies and hardships of life in New York's slums. Some sent money, others came to offer their time and help.

But not everyone supported them. Certain clerics in the hierarchy saw the Catholic Worker movement as nothing more than a Red ploy to infiltrate the Church. Even the FBI got involved, in time accumulating a file of five hundred pages about *The Catholic Worker.* They were trying to classify what kind of "subversion" those dedicated men and women (God's underground movement in America) were up to.

The Catholic Worker house also offered talks on faith and works, as well as leading Catholic issues. These talks were usually given in the basement of the Worker house or in a rented hall. Many famous Catholics of the time came to speak, among them Jesuits such as Father John La Farge, philosophers such as Jacques Maritain, and poets such as the Englishman Hilaire Belloc.

All commented on the courage and goodwill of the Catholic Workers, the movement's founders, and its many volunteers. Newcomers were often surprised on meeting the founder. Dorothy wore no makeup and dressed in secondhand clothes, her hair in braids wound around her head. But her dynamic presence assured everyone that she was indeed in charge.

One of the most devoted workers was a seventeen-year-old student, Stanley Vishnewski. After reading about *The Catholic Worker* in the *Brooklyn Register,* Stanley walked across the Brooklyn Bridge to find the Worker House. He stayed with the movement until his death at sixty-three. Other young students and idealistic Catholics were also inspired to join the Workers and care for the poor.

Because Communists were working to attract Blacks to their cause, Dorothy wanted to make sure that people of other races would feel welcome in the Worker movement as well. In 1934 she wrote to the publisher of the *Brooklyn Tablet:* "Please announce in your paper that we are sponsoring a Catholic Interracial Mass Meeting, the first to be held in the East. Father James Gillis, a champion of Black people, will be the main speaker."

The meeting was such a success that Dorothy opened a second house of hospitality in Harlem. Classes were held in a storefront for the Harlem children. Volunteers read to them and taught useful crafts such as sewing. Some of the volunteers were students at Cathedral High School. One, after meeting Dorothy, described her as tall, slender, well-spoken, and vigorous, with a long stride. She was a born leader.

CHAPTER EIGHT

GARDEN COMMUNES

Staten Island offered the closest rural life to Manhattan. It was only a five-cent ferry ride away. It was also a place much loved by Dorothy, who still owned her beach cottage there.

In the second issue of *The Catholic Worker*, Peter Maurin wrote an article about the benefits of farming as being good for the body as well as the soul. He wrote that the best way to help the indigent was to have them live in community, working and praying together. So began their first experiment—a twelve-room house that Dorothy rented on Staten Island. Her vision was to run a farm and school combined. Peter called the place an agronomic university where "workers could be scholars and scholars workers."

The house had a wide, wraparound porch and sat on a high knoll overlooking Raritan Bay. At the first signs of spring, enthusiastic young volunteers took the ferry to Staten Island and set to work cultivating the land. Others hammered and painted to make the old house habitable. Due to plenty of rain that summer of 1935, the amateur farmers raised a giant crop of vegetables and fruit.

That same year *The Catholic Worker* moved from 15th Street to a four-story house at 144 Charles Street. The upper floors were used as the house of hospitality, the lower floors for the office.

With rumors crossing the Atlantic about Hitler and anti-Semitism, Dorothy was furious. She led a group that demonstrated in front of the German Embassy near the Battery. Another time she took college students to picket the *Bremen,* a German ocean liner with a swastika painted on its bow.

But as fast as Dorothy and her group distributed leaflets condemning the Nazis, Peter Maurin picked them up. One of his beliefs was that Christians must obey authorities, a precept straight from the Bible. Littering was against the law.

More and more people began reading *The Catholic Worker.* Each month bundles of the paper were shipped to churches, monasteries, parochial schools, and universities. Many Catholic students were inspired to give their time to the radical movement. They distributed the newspaper at Union Square, at Times Square, and around Madison Square Garden. "It is the man in the street we need to reach," emphasized Dorothy.

Her fame spread. Newspaper and magazine journalists wrote articles about the amazing woman who claimed to be a Catholic while behaving like a Communist. In addition to being a talented writer, Dorothy was an inspiring speaker who never used notes. She was invited to appear before churches and campuses all over the country. In order to save money, she rode Greyhound buses to her far-off engagements and slept anywhere provided. The bus rides gave her a bit of quiet, during which she answered some of the thousands of letters that arrived monthly. Many were cries for help, many were fan letters. Dorothy rarely answered the outpourings of praise, complaining, "I wake up with letters to answer and go to bed with letters to answer. I even carry a bundle of letters with me everywhere I go." But she did keep up a voluminous correspondence with people she valued.

With her busy schedule and constant traveling, Dorothy turned the care of eight-year-old Tamar over to Steve and Mary Johnson, Catholic Workers who ran the Garden Commune on Staten Island. She gave them her little beach cottage to live in. There Tamar attended a nearby school. During the Christmas holidays, Tamar went "home" to be with her mother, but being in the hospitality house also meant she lived among crazed men and women, derelicts, and alcoholics. Later she attended St. Patrick's Boarding School on Staten Island, where she was a mediocre student. Tamar was always a quiet, good child who took whatever life dished out. Dorothy observed that her greatest sacrifice in life was being separated from her child.

In April 1936, the Catholic Workers moved to Mott Street in Chinatown. The place consisted of two buildings, one behind the other, both constructed before the Civil War. The front building was used to publish the newspaper and for business offices. The rear building became the hospitality house. Both were dirty, vermin-infested, cold, and damp. Dorothy called this uninviting place home for the next fifteen years, using two rooms on the top floor as her apartment, and from here traveling across the country.

On one tour to the deep South, Dorothy fell into great danger. She went to Memphis, Tennessee, to support the Southern Tenant Farmers Union. It had been organized by Protestant ministers to help poor Black sharecroppers. Dorothy and the Black clergy left on a freezing cold morning to deliver food, coffee, and soap to the striking farmers. The group arrived in Parker, Arkansas, to discover a hundred poor Blacks living in unheated tents in the snow. The men had been evicted from their wooden shacks because of their union activity. The men asked the U.S. Government to help them start a few cooperative farms.

Touched by their misery and hopelessness, Dorothy sent a telegram to then First Lady Eleanor Roosevelt explaining the farmers' plight. Mrs. Roosevelt replied, asking the Arkansas Governor to do something immediately. But for her effort, Dorothy was called a Communist and a busybody. After she visited a farmer's shack, masked riders attacked the place and shot the helpless man. Dorothy was grazed by a bullet.

Peter Maurin did not approve of men working for wages or using strikes to get higher salaries. He wanted a society where all work was a gift, not a commodity. Meanwhile Dorothy used her newspaper to support strikers at the Borden Milk Company as well as at Orbach's, a dress store on 14th Street. She even sent Catholic Workers to picket the store, and the union won!

The year 1936 saw still another extension of the Catholic Worker movement. From the beginning, Peter had talked of an "agronomic" university or community farm. He and Dorothy felt Christians should live in community as they did in the first century. But that type of life required many sacrifices: sacrifice of privacy, quiet, ownership, and the chance to acquire wealth. All of these Dorothy and Peter had given up long ago themselves with the start of the Catholic Worker movement. But what of the other people they needed to help make the idea real? Where would they get the money to buy a farm for this community?

Unexpectedly, Grace Branham, a retired school-teacher, offered her savings of $1,000 to the Workers to buy a farm. There was one condition: that they build her a small house on the property where she could retire.

Dorothy and Peter borrowed a car and took off, looking for a place to buy. Eventually they found an old farm outside Easton, Pennsylvania. Its rickety house sat on a hill overlooking thirty much-worn acres. The road up to the house was washed out and full of ruts. But the place was only seventy-five miles from New York City, and the price was exactly one thousand dollars. Peter beamed when he saw the place; his lifelong dream was about to come true! That March Dorothy finalized the purchase of the Easton property.

One clear, bright day in mid-April, Dorothy, Peter, Tamar, and two strong young men from Mott Street piled into the car to take over the place. During the seventy-five-mile drive everyone chatted excitedly about future plans for their new community.

After driving two hours they turned off Highway 22 and Dorothy called out, pointing, "There it is. That old house at the crest of the hill."

Everyone craned to get a view from the car windows. Some looked pleased, others disappointed.

"How do we get up there?" Tamar asked.

"Hold on everyone, here we go," Dorothy laughed, pressing her foot hard on the pedal. The car shot upward, rocking from side to side like a rowboat in a storm. Suddenly the car stopped.

"I think we're stuck in a ditch," exclaimed Peter, in his French accent.

"Everyone out!" ordered Dorothy. "Push the car hard. Let's go. One, two, three, push!" After a few tries, the old car straightened out and continued on its way, bumping and lurching. At last it stopped in front of the decrepit farmhouse.

"What a beautiful view," each exclaimed, as they gazed across the valley.

"Come on, Tamar," called Dorothy, "let's look inside." They entered the dark, gloomy, front room.

"Where's the light?" asked Tamar, squinting in the shadows.

"There isn't any," Dorothy replied. "We're too far from town for electricity. Here's an old kerosene lamp." She fumbled for her cigarette lighter. Suddenly the lamp flickered, shedding a small circle of yellow around the room. The kitchen held rickety old-fashioned furnishings, including a corrugated metal sink and an ancient wood-burning stove.

"Where's *my* room?" asked Tamar, running up the stairs. From above she called, "There are loads of bedrooms up here. Can I have any one I want?"

Not wanting to dampen her child's pleasure, Dorothy answered, "Sure." But she knew there would always be so many "guests" at the house that she and Tamar would have to sleep on cots in the hall.

Peter wasn't interested in the house. He was tramping over the thirty acres, imagining them covered with crops and planted with enough vegetables to feed the city-dwellers who came to share "hospitality." Peter looked over the dilapidated barn. "Once we fix this up, we must have a cow," he stated.

"And pigs and chickens," squealed Tamar, who loved animals.

There was a great amount of work to be done before the summer "guests" arrived. Every weekend, groups of young people drove down to Easton to hammer and saw, hoe and rake, scrape and paint. By June everything was ready for the big move.

There was one hitch: most of the visitors were from the city and knew nothing about farming or the care of animals. Also, the "guests" were used to canned and packaged foods and resisted eating fresh vegetables. Peter wanted the farm to be self-sufficient, but the residents complained about the homegrown vegetables and lack of meat. The bickering went on all summer, sometimes ending in fistfights. This caused Peter great pain as he was against any form of violence.

Dorothy wanted the farm to accept anyone who came for help. The farm was used as a camp for inner-city kids, providing relief from the summer heat for children from Harlem. It was also a "religious university" for priests who came to hear Peter speak, always delivering his point with the emphasis of a waving index finger. And the farm was used as a home for indigents. Invalids, the crippled, the homeless—all came for their turn in the fresh air. Most couldn't or wouldn't work, and no one forced them to. Dorothy, Peter, and dedicated volunteers took care of their needs. For all it was a place of quiet and reflection. At 9:00 P.M. everyone came together in the main room of "Mary Farm," as Dorothy called it, to recite the rosary and litany.

Tamar loved Mary Farm where she was free to run and play all summer and be with her mother, to whom she clung with adoring abandon. Steve and Mary Johnson, who cared for Tamar on Staten Island, also came to Easton during the summers to watch her when Dorothy was away giving speeches. Many people criticized the single mother for the haphazard manner in which she raised her daughter. But the little girl seemed happy and healthy, although she was very quiet and shy. She also did not do well during the year when she attended St. Patrick's school on Staten Island. Summers were best for her when she could be at Mary Farm. When Tamar was fifteen, Dorothy enrolled her in an unusual school in Canada. There students were trained in farming, spinning, weaving, knitting, and making butter and cheese. It was not much of a preparation for modern life, but Tamar always enjoyed Mary Farm and hoped to marry a farmer.

From the very beginning, funds to run the farm came from dedicated subscribers to *The Catholic Worker.* Whenever money ran out, Dorothy printed a heart-rending appeal in the paper. Soon after the appeal, checks and cash would arrive. She supported both the farm and her city house this way. At the Mott Street building, each morning a long line of indigent men shuffled toward the Worker house to receive coffee and bread. As the depression worsened, the line grew longer, until every day a thousand men waited patiently for what often was their only food of the day. Dorothy's articles in *The Catholic Worker* begged for help. She wrote, "We are $1200 in debt for food. We owe $400 towards the last month's printing bill." Another issue stated, "Our electricity is about to be shut off." Her loyal readers always came through. One sent 10¢, another a check for $100. When things became desperate, she went on tour. Her speaking engagements not only brought in fees, but also spread the word about the Catholic Worker movement.

As gifted as she was, Dorothy hated speaking before a large audience. Each time she felt sick to her stomach and nervous. But it had to be done. Fundraising was a major part of her Christian mission, but it cost her physically. She always returned to Mott Street or the Easton farm totally exhausted. The only part of travel she enjoyed was the quiet hours on the bus where she could read undisturbed.

In 1939 Dorothy's father died alone in a New York hotel. His ashes were scattered over the Hialeah racetrack that he had founded. To the end, John Day thought of Dorothy as the "nut of the family."

But the "nut" was doing very well. In 1938 her book *From Union Square to Rome* was published. It was an autobiographical explanation of her conversion to Catholicism. One reviewer criticized Dorothy, calling her transformation a distorted desire to be with the poor and the abandoned, and dismissing her as just a radical who became a Catholic. But a prisoner who had once

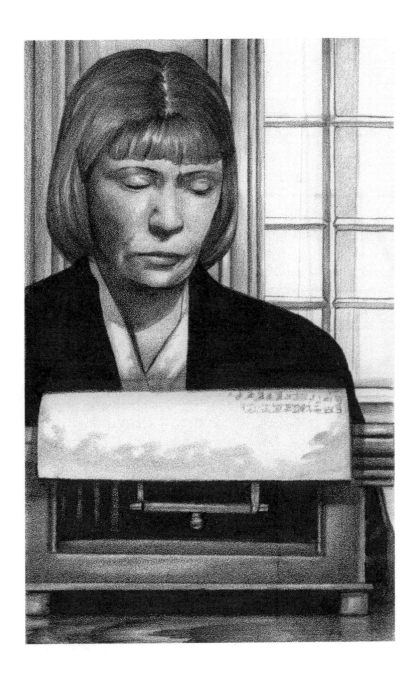

enjoyed her hospitality at Mott Street was kinder. He wrote he often prayed that God would send thousands of Dorothys and Peters to show the world how Christians should love each other.

Between her books and speaking tours, Dorothy was becoming a celebrity. People came from everywhere to discuss their hopes and spiritual problems with her. By then in her forties, Dorothy yearned for privacy and quiet, some time of her own. It became harder to find. The stress brought on headaches, even pains in her heart. But there were forty more years ahead to continue her pilgrimage.

World War II brought a new aspect to her Christian witness, an uncompromising witness for peace. She had protested World War I, the draft, and the jailing of conscientious objectors. But World War I had had many dissenters and she was not a lone voice. World War II, however, was a "popular" war. Young Catholic men enlisted in droves, and families were engulfed in patriotism. Now, despite being one of the most influential lay people in the American Catholic Church, Dorothy Day was out of step with mainstream Catholics.

Her articles in *The Catholic Worker* were all against support of the war and the military. As a result the paper's circulation fell dramatically. Many Worker houses closed. Letters poured in, many of them abusive, saying she obviously did not understand what the war was about; America's young men were fighting to save democracy and to rescue the Jews.

Even when the Japanese attacked Pearl Harbor, which catapulted America into the war, Dorothy did not change her stand. Still, she was affected by the war's impact. With young Catholics enlisting or being drafted, there were fewer and fewer volunteers to help at Worker houses. Soon there were not enough people to write, ship, and sell the newspaper. Contributions of food and money dried up. One month the electricity was shut off at Mott Street when she couldn't pay the bill. In 1938, *The Catholic Worker* had had 190,000 subscribers; by the close of the war in 1945, the count would be down to 25,000.

But Dorothy had unlimited faith and expectations and believed God would come through for her. Her greatest power lay in her faith. She discovered a new way of deepening that faith and her fellowship with God through the retreat movement.

CHAPTER NINE

THE RETREAT MOVEMENT

In 1940 *The Catholic Worker* advertised a three-day "silent retreat." It was to be held over Labor Day, and Father Paul Hanley Furfey of Catholic University would be the retreat conductor. Dorothy wanted the retreat to be silent, penitential, and life changing. And it was.

Over a hundred young people attended, with the overflow housed in tents and the barn. This retreat made such a deep impression on her that she mentioned it repeatedly for years to come. And with its great success, she planned another for the following year. In fact, these deeply spiritual Catholic Worker retreats would be held regularly for the next twenty-five years.

The second retreat was led by a young priest, Father John Hugo. This retreat made an even deeper impression on Dorothy, so that afterwards she dropped much of her brassiness and became gentler and softer. She even gave up smoking and her tough newsroom language. She mellowed, seeming almost another person. Father Hugo, a professor at Mount Mercy College in Pittsburgh, became her spiritual director and remained so until her death.

That same summer of 1941, Tamar returned from school in Canada to help at Mary Farm. Her mother was quite firm about how she was to spend her vacation. "If you are sick, stay in bed," Dorothy commanded, "but if well, I expect you to do your share of work."

Much as Tamar liked farming and animals, she now found a greater interest at Easton. It was Dave Hennessy, a young volunteer who was to become her husband. Like all mothers, Dorothy was concerned about her only child's future. Dave had no degree, no nest egg, and no real career. But Tamar was in love and with the usual blindness of young love saw none of this. Perhaps mindful of the many mistakes she herself had made in her youth, Dorothy decided to end the budding romance by sending Tamar away from Easton to a school in Newport, Rhode Island.

Dorothy made an appointment with Forster, Tamar's father, and let him know what was taking place. Although Dorothy and Forster never married, he always took an interest in the affairs of his daughter and helped finance her schooling.

When Dorothy visited Newport to help celebrate Tamar's seventeenth birthday, she discovered that Dave Hennessy had been writing her there. He even wrote letters to Dorothy, which she considered rude. Father Hugo told her, "It is no use opposing the marriage." But she tried everything to stop it, ordering Tamar to wait a year until she turned eighteen.

Tamar never graduated from high school, as she didn't have sufficient credits. Dorothy then registered her at an agricultural school in Farmingdale on Long Island. She herself took a room in a nearby convent where she planned to live the life of a hermit. She needed to grow spiritually, as well as to escape the busyness of her life. It was a relentless burden to keep the Catholic Worker paper, houses, and farm running, a burden made all the more exhausting by the constant whining and complaining workers about who was and wasn't doing their share. The convent provided Dorothy with some needed rest, as well as a close and convenient spot from which to keep an eye on her daughter.

Tamar turned eighteen on March 4, 1944. And despite her mother's efforts, just a few weeks later she became Mrs. Dave Hennessy. Wearing a simple wedding gown made by her Aunt Tessa, Dorothy's sister-in-law, Tamar was wed at 8:00 A.M. in St. Bernard's Church in Easton. The newlyweds and guests celebrated afterwards with a wedding breakfast cooked by one of the men who worked on the farm. Then the young couple settled into a shack filled with tormenting bedbugs. Tamar's married life was never to get much better.

Over the years, Dorothy found her deepest spiritual health during retreats at convents and monasteries. But even those periods of silence didn't entirely free her from the bickering and fighting that went on continually between families and guests living on the Easton property. To solve that problem, she decided to change Mary Farm into a retreat center with Father Hugo as its resident chaplain. But her personal problems with her daughter continued to weigh on her.

By then Tamar had given birth to her first child, Rebecca. One after the other, seven more children would follow. Dorothy felt that the Hennessys needed to break away from her control and have a farm of their own. Forster gave his daughter a check for $1,000 as a down payment, and in 1947 Tamar and David found a place in Berkeley Springs, West Virginia, on seventy-five acres. The full price was only $2,500. The house had plenty of space for the expanding Hennessy family, but with no comforts or luxuries. It needed a lot of work. To pay for the repairs, Dorothy gave Tamar the cash advance from a newly sold book. With that, the farm was completely Tamar's.

Tamar was not the only one to move. Next came big changes for the Catholic Worker. One morning a worker at the Mott Street house brought Dorothy the mail.

"What's this?" she asked, her eyes almost pleading for "no more problems," a hopeless wish.

"It's from the landlady," he answered. "She's selling the Mott Street houses."

Dorothy put her head in her hands, her iron-gray braid coming loose. "Where can we go?" she moaned. "Who would rent to us, a household of drunks, crazies, and former prostitutes?" The worker wasn't fazed. "Well," he suggested, "if we can't rent, why not buy a place!" Dorothy raised her head. Her blue eyes sparkled. "Then nobody can turn us out. Ever!" she exclaimed.

She immediately got on the phone. First she contacted a realtor friend, who was a regular supporter of the Catholic Worker movement. The next issue of the paper contained a plea for someone to find them a place to move, plus a fairy godmother to pay for it. They needed at least $25,000 to get a new house. By the date the residents of Mott Street were required to move, the problem had been solved.

Dorothy discovered a much nicer, more modern house at 223 Chrystie Street. It had a wrought iron fence, a small yard, and real bathrooms, a first for the Catholic Workers. Dorothy's friend Madeline Krider provided the money for a down payment, and the Workers moved in.

A few years later, in 1947, Dorothy sold the Easton farm and invested the money in a better retreat center in Newburgh, an hour's train ride from New York City. Right on the Hudson River, it had a large stone house set in acres of fine lush farmland. It became a popular retreat center for the next eight years.

Each summer until 1955, a priest came to conduct six-day retreats at Newburgh. Many priests and religious turned up at Newburgh, as well as lay people, all of them searching for answers and solutions to their problems. Small groups met for discussion under the shady trees.

Those summers were wonderful and uplifting, while the farm produced enough food for the thirty-five or more retreatants. There was also enough left over to ship down to the breadline on Chrystie Street.

Dorothy enjoyed the retreats. She took lengthy notes of the instructions in a ruled notebook, reading the spiritual words over and over, honoring each as a gift. "They have a distilled sweetness," she claimed, "like a drop of precious ointment." But not every retreat brought her to such spiritual heights. Some just bored her to death.

During this time, Dorothy suffered the loss of Peter Maurin, co-founder of the Catholic Worker movement. He was twenty years older than she. A social radical to the end, Peter had traveled the country preaching on the need for hospitality, utopian agrarian communities, and education through dialogue. As he approached his seventieth birthday, he began to lose his memory, and probably suffered a stroke. Soon he could no longer teach or preach. He became incontinent and had to be fed, dressed, and undressed. All day he sat in a chair, wrapped in blankets, just staring into space, remaining silent for the last years of his life. In May 1949 he developed a severe cough and died at the farm in Newburgh on May 15. His funeral was at the church on Mott Street, and he was buried in Queens. Dorothy was in Ohio when she received word of Peter's death. She left immediately, arriving in time to attend his funeral. His death was a terrible blow to her, but she knew her old friend was in a better place.

She later honored him in a unique way. She'd been working on an autobiography that included her conversion; the book was called *The Long Loneliness*. It was published in 1952 by Harper and Brothers, a very important publisher. She used the $1,000 advance for a down payment on a new retreat center on Staten Island, which she named in honor of her friend, calling it the Peter Maurin Farm.

Dorothy had never imagined that so much of her time would be spent in buying and selling property. But the poor needed places to stay and be fed, and young Catholics needed spiritual strength from retreats. As balance to the financial dealings, Dorothy delighted in being a grandmother. Each time Tamar had another baby, Dorothy went to West Virginia to help with the delivery and to care for the other children. She had only one daughter, and the two had been separated during most of Tamar's childhood.

At last she had time to enjoy the brood of Hennessy children, which kept getting bigger every year. However, she did regret Tamar's poverty. The heavy work on the farm was unending, plus there was the care of so many little ones. Always thin and frail, Tamar looked increasingly tired, almost wasting away. Dorothy yearned to relieve her daughter's burden. She sent checks to the Hennessys whenever she received a royalty on a book or sold an article. They needed so much. Tamar pretended to be happy, but the sad situation wore heavily on Dorothy.

Then Dave Hennessy ran off, leaving Tamar to handle everything herself. The chimney of their house was cracked, the roof was leaking, the barn was collapsing, sinks were stopped up, and still the children had to be raised. The stress had been just too much for Dave, who was suffering from a nervous disorder and probably had a mental breakdown. He was no longer able to face the support of a wife and eight children, the care of a farm, and no money. But in running off, he left his wife to do everything alone.

In 1952, a friend drove the Hennessy children to Staten Island where Dorothy at first cared for them at the Peter Maurin Farm, then later moved the family to a rental house. Tamar seemed to be happy and able to cope with her new situation as a single mother. Dorothy loved having her nearby and continued to

help her financially, but she also felt guilty. She felt certain that she had been too forceful with Tamar and Dave and perhaps had usurped his position as the family leader. The breakup of Tamar's marriage was a heavy cross Dorothy would bear for the rest of her life.

CHAPTER TEN

REBEL WITH MANY CAUSES

During her teens, Dorothy Day had marched and fasted for various causes. She continued this practice into her seventies. If there was a genuine need, if giving of herself could help others, she was never too weak or too old to participate. She was always ready to take a stand for any cause she believed in.

In her midlife years, her main focus was on peace—peace in the world, peace in people's hearts. Another of her causes was supporting unions; unions gave workers security in their jobs and provided health and death benefits. Also, she fought for the rights of all people, regardless of race.

On a cross-country bus trip during World War II, she visited a concentration camp in California where families of Japanese heritage were interned. The United States feared Japanese-Americans might help Hirohito's forces invade our country. Dorothy wrote in *The Catholic Worker*, "We must cry out against this injustice." She was also moved by the plight of Mexican-American grape pickers in California, led by Cesar Chavez. Closer to home was a strike against New York's Cardinal Spellman by the gravediggers of Calvary Cemetery. Dorothy was in awe of God, but not of the cardinal. She asked her

Catholic Workers to join the strikers as the picketers marched around St. Patrick's Cathedral on Fifth Avenue. Local Catholics expected her to be struck down by God for defying such an important cleric.

Despite all her activities, Dorothy was often lonely, even in the noisy, crowded Worker houses. Then, unexpectedly, during a December bus trip in 1949, she was met at the station in Phoenix by Ammon Hennacy. Hennacy was a Baptist who fasted and picketed for social causes and who, like Dorothy, was often arrested for his actions. She hadn't seen him since 1938 when he had attended a lecture she had given at Marquette University in Milwaukee, Wisconsin.

Hennacy was very impressed by what Dorothy had done over the years, and he returned to New York with her. He became deeply involved in the Worker movement. He wrote for the paper, helped run the house, and made it quite plain that he was in love with its founder. He showed his devotion by presenting her with a rose or writing affectionate notes.

Dorothy was in her fifties, and no man had shown a romantic interest in her since her conversion. It was very difficult for the lonely, middle-aged woman to turn Ammon away. He was tall and masculine with strong features and thick dark hair. She accepted some of his affection, hoping it would lead not to marriage, but to Ammon's baptism in the Catholic Church. Though a Protestant, Ammon gave his life and service to Catholic action. He underwent long fasts, participated in strikes and marches, even made posters and banners to carry as he marched in Dorothy's various demonstrations. He finally became a Catholic in 1952, with Dorothy as his godmother.

Following the defeat of Hitler's Nazis, America was obsessed with a new fear: Communism. The United States' participation in the Korean War kept employment high and the need for shelter low. Food lines were short. Many Catholic Worker houses around the country closed. Some people said the movement was over.

Dorothy was deeply hurt. She thought that there was too much talk of raising up leaders, and not enough talk of raising up servants. She also considered the Catholic Worker movement to still be one of the most important in the country.

When young men began to return from their service in the Korean War, or were released from conscientious objector camps, they wanted to give their lives to something that was uplifting and worthwhile. Their idealism produced a reawakening of the Catholic Worker movement, and the movement began to refocus its attention on peace.

And peace was needed. Though the United States was not in a "shooting war," it was engaged in a strong conflict with the Soviets. Called the "Cold War," this conflict encompassed politics, economics, philosophy, even the culture of the different countries. Put simply, the United Sates believed the Soviets ruled by totalitarian and dictatorship, while the Soviets said the United States had corrupted democracy with capitalism and was interfering with countries where its presence was not wanted.

Increasing the tensions of the conflict, the Soviets produced an atom bomb as well as the missiles to deliver it. No longer was the United States protected by its vast oceans. An intercontinental ballistic missile with a nuclear warhead could be launched in Russia and in an hour destroy any American city. The United States responded with its own build-up of weapons.

With the Cold War came the McCarthy Era, named for Senator Joseph McCarthy who investigated anyone who might be a Communist. During the early 1950s, anyone with leftist leanings, or who had engaged in "suspicious" activities even decades earlier, was labeled a Red or a pinko and considered a spy. These people were called to Washington to appear before the Un-American Activities Committee to defend themselves. Even innocent people became suspect and were called before the Committee. Just to be called tainted one's reputation, and in this way McCarthy ruined the reputations of movie stars, authors, politicians, professors, and journalists. In the rest of the country, a fear of anything Russian and a sense of hysteria and impending doom seized the hearts and minds of once-rational Americans. Bomb shelters were constructed, and bomb drills were ordered in expectation of Russian attacks. Residents of big cities like New York were required to leave their home or office at the sound of a siren and scurry to underground shelters.

Always the rebel, Dorothy refused to go. She was against war and all methods of war. In her support of peace, she included loving Russians. When the air-raid alarms sounded, Dorothy and Ammon Hennacy, plus many of her Worker family, defiantly sat on park benches in nearby Washington Square or City Hall Park refusing to move. Each time, Dorothy and her supporters were arrested, handcuffed, and carted off to jail for breaking the law. Dorothy didn't mind going to jail; actually, she found it quite restful. During the ten-day sentences she had no responsibilities, no work, and lots of time to pray and think. But her actions just added to the growing file the FBI was compiling on her and her newspaper.

As the fifties passed, two new issues arose that took much of her time and prayers. These were the Vietnam War and the Civil Rights movement.

Dorothy was genuinely sympathetic to the plight of Blacks in the South. Southern Blacks lived in constant fear of their white neighbors, especially the Ku Klux Klan. Many Blacks were beaten, hung, and even burned alive. Here was a cause that literally screamed for her help.

Clarence Jordan, a White Baptist minister, had started a communal farm in Georgia called *Koinonia.* It was run much like the Worker farms in Newburgh and Staten Island. Jordan and his fellow workers were in great danger because Jordan had opened Koinonia to both Blacks and Whites. This was against Georgia law, which required segregation of the races. As a result, Koinonia suffered several attacks by local segregationists.

In April 1956 Dorothy took a bus to Americus, Georgia, to lend her support to the group. The day before Easter, she was assigned to wait in a station wagon outside the entrance to Koinonia and to act as a lookout. At midnight a car full of white supremacists sped past the entrance, shooting toward the station wagon. At the first shot, Dorothy slid down to the floor of the car and wasn't injured. But her brush with death showed how dangerous it was to be a rebel in the South. It was in the

South that she had been shot at years before, helping black sharecroppers.

Despite her travels, problems with the Chrystie Street settlement still occupied her. As one example, many of the Workers and "residents" at the Chrystie Street house were smokers. Some of the indigents were mentally ill or alcoholics. One night a drunken resident left a burning cigarette in a chair. Before long the entire house was on fire. Though everyone else escaped, an elderly man died of smoke inhalation.

Dorothy was blamed for the incident. Inspection showed the place to be without a sprinkler system and to have several blocked exits, which prevented escape. Called to appear in court, she was scolded by the judge. He said to her, "It is not charity to house people in a fire-trap," and ordered the place closed immediately.

That afternoon a reporter from the *New York Times* phoned her. She told him that the judge had fined her and ordered everyone evicted from the Chrystie Street house. The reporter was horrified. He rushed downtown to see the damage and to talk things over with Dorothy. Later that afternoon the reporter spoke to the judge, explaining the situation. Where would all the street people sleep that night? How would the hungry be fed? The next morning the judge rescinded his order to evacuate the house and only required that a sprinkler system be installed.

Somehow the story made various nightly TV shows. Viewers saw Dorothy as a gray-haired woman who was only valiantly trying to feed and house the poor. The story touched the hearts of people all over America. Letters filled with contributions poured in, enough to fireproof the building and install the required sprinklers. An added advantage to the news story was that the Worker movement became nationally known.

Several years later, in 1958, the Chrystie Street house was ordered closed again when New York City decided to expand its subway system. The house was directly in its path. Dorothy was offered $27,000 for the property. The money sounded great, but where would she publish *The Catholic Worker,* where house her crowd of indigents? Everyone was ordered to vacate by August.

First Dorothy rented an old loft on Spring Street. Though it was unsatisfactory, the paper ended up remaining there for two years. The old loft had no sleeping quarters, so she had to rent places for the homeless men to sleep. When the check for the $27,000 finally arrived, she paid off the mortgage of the Peter Maurin Farm on Staten Island and invested the rest in two nearby beach cottages.

The year 1958 also brought two celebrations—the 25th anniversary of *The Catholic Worker,* the circulation of which was back up again to 100,000, and the election of a new Catholic Pope, John XXIII. Dorothy wondered what changes the former Cardinal of Venice would bring to the Church, never imagining what would actually happen in the wake of Vatican II.

Dorothy's immediate area also underwent changes. Staten Island had more residents, more traffic, and more pollution blowing in from factories along the New Jersey shore. To get Tamar and her children away from the congestion, Dorothy bought her daughter an old farmhouse in Vermont. Its twelve large rooms appealed to everyone. Dorothy helped the Hennessys move from the cottage to Perkinsville, Vermont, glad to see them in a place big enough for such a large family.

But as always, Dorothy's personal life took a back seat to her efforts for peace and justice. Though Joseph McCarthy himself had been discredited years earlier, and his witch hunt investigating American citizens was long over, Communism itself still posed the real threat of nuclear war. In the early 1960s, the United States began to feel terrorized by the closeness of Communist Cuba. Then the Russians erected missiles in Cuba. Only ninety miles south of Florida's Key West, the missiles were aimed at American cities. Nuclear war seemed imminent. School children across the entire country regularly had air-raid drills in which they were taught to hide under their desks and cover their heads. Wealthy families built concrete bomb shelters in their backyards. Others stored canned goods and paper products in suitcases, ready to carry them to safety. But, of course, there was no escape from an atomic bomb.

In 1962 Dorothy decided to go to Cuba on a mission of peace. She wanted to talk to President Fidel Castro, who was responsible for allowing the rockets to be in Cuba. After all, Fidel and his brother Raoul were cradle Catholics, and they were idealistic Communists. Fidel had fought as a guerrilla soldier to overturn the reign of dictator Fulgencio Batista and to bring economic development to the people of Cuba. Though now aligned with the Russian Soviets, surely Castro, she reasoned, still cared about the poor and oppressed as she did.

Once the pearl of the Caribbean, Havana was now
run-down and shabby, its streets empty. There was not
enough food or medicine. Cuban funds went to military
equipment and soldiers. The country had become an
armed camp, just miles from the U.S. border.

Americans were not allowed to travel to Cuba. So
Dorothy obtained a visa from the Czechoslovakian
Embassy and sailed to Havana aboard a Spanish ship.

While in Cuba, she never actually met Castro, only
getting a glimpse of the Communist dictator from afar.
Instead she saw parades, flags, and banners, and went
on the restricted tours foreigners were allowed to take.
Later she took buses to other parts of the island, visiting
small, primitive villages. After a month she returned
home by way of Mexico.

Dorothy seemed to defend Castro, writing that it
was better to revolt and fight as he did with his hand-
ful of men, than to do nothing. A flood of letters
poured in from angry readers, protesting her visit and
accusing her of turning a blind eye to Cuba's failures,
its closed churches, its imprisoned clergy, and its
forced labor. They accused her of abandoning pacifi-
cism to support violent revolt. Dorothy said that these
claims were nonsense. She recognized the revolution's faults but was always more interested in the
spiritual state of the country, hoping that a radical
Christianity would ultimately emerge from it.

The following summer, in 1963, Dorothy decided to
make a pilgrimage for peace to Rome. She was pleased
with John XXIII, who had been pope for about five years
by then. A rotund, smiling man, he was immensely popular. One of his first major acts was to call a Vatican

Council, a gathering of clergy and key people from around the world. Their purpose was to modernize the church, to promote Christian unity, and to increase the holiness of all Catholics, both laity and clergy.

Dorothy received no special invitation to the Council, or even a private audience with John XXIII, while she was there. She traveled as an ordinary tourist, with friends paying for her ticket. She admired the sites of ancient Rome, the tombs of various saints, and the Vatican. During a public audience in St. Peter's, the pope acknowledged various pilgrim groups. He expressed gratitude and encouragement in particular for the "Pilgrims for Peace," as her group was called, saying their message brought comfort to his heart. Then he gave the group his blessing and asked them to continue to work for peace.

Dorothy returned to New York. By now she had lost Ammon Hennacy, who had given up both Catholicism and any hope of winning her hand. She had also lost much of her beauty. Her braids were white, her cosmetic-free face was deeply wrinkled, and the results of her hard life were clearly visible.

One place Dorothy found rest was in a new Catholic Worker retreat. New York was building a huge new bridge to connect Brooklyn, Staten Island, and New Jersey. It was to be called the Verrazano Bridge, named for the Italian explorer. The Peter Maurin Farm, bought years before for $16,000, was suddenly worth many times that, as its land was required for the bridge. Dorothy was offered $100,000 for the farm. At last she had enough to buy a really fine retreat center. She looked at many available properties and settled on Tivoli, the former estate of the de Peyster family, near Bard College. The property was situated in the township of Red Hook, ninety miles north of New York City. Standing on the east shore of the Hudson River looking toward the Catskill Mountains, it consisted of twenty-five beautifully landscaped acres with many garden paths. The three large stone houses, perfect for summertime retreats and vacations, had been used before as a school and as a summer camp, as well as an orphanage. The buildings were run-down and dilapidated, but by now the Catholic Workers were long used to repairing and renovating. Soon the place was open to the homeless, a large percentage of which were also alcoholic. In later years Tivoli also opened a day-care program for the many migrant workers who traveled to New York to work its apple orchards.

In 1962, a group of Catholics formed the American PAX Association (later to become the U.S. branch of Pax Christi). Dorothy Day became a member, as well as such other well-known Catholics as Thomas Merton. In 1964, PAX held its first peace conference at Tivoli. It was the time of the unpopular Vietnam War. During the Tivoli conferences, young people were trained in nonviolent methods for obtaining peace. Musicians, writers, artists, pacifist leaders, and outstanding intellectuals from around the world all made Tivoli their meeting place and cultural center. Lectures, poetry readings, folk dances, and movies were presented. Dorothy enjoyed the summers at Tivoli as much as the visitors. These were the happiest of times for her, fulfilling all she had dreamed of for the Catholic Worker movement.

Dorothy was revered and honored as the movement's co-founder. Her books, mostly about herself and her spiritual journey, were accepted by major publishers. She became the most influential lay Catholic in the history of American Catholicism. Her life and work helped change the concept of laity from passive observers to dedicated doers of the Word. Millions greatly admired her courage, humility, and persistence. True, nuns such as Mother Cabrini and Mother Teresa had cared about the poor, but here was a laywoman, a divorcée, a single mother—someone with a successful career as a journalist and author—who had given up everything such success might have brought her, to instead share the dirt, lice, stench, and endless miseries of God's urban poor. Only a woman of guts and extraordinary commitment could have endured such voluntary poverty.

But all this activity had not been restricted solely to Dorothy Day's youth. Nearing seventy and troubled by heart murmurs and arthritis, she still found the strength to travel, even to fast. In 1965 she flew to Rome for the third session of the Vatican Council, along with her friend Eileen Egan (best known for her work with and about Mother Teresa). The two were part of an international group of twenty Catholic women who hoped to influence the Council to make a statement against war and to support those who refused to serve in any branch of the military. The women intended to bring attention to their request with a ten-day fast.

In Rome, until the day the fast began, Dorothy met with bishops and people active in peace movements. Then the twenty women moved into a convent near St. Peter's where they would live during the ten days. Dorothy offered her fast for peace and "in part for the victims of famine all over the world." She had fasted before, but was surprised by the extreme pain she suffered this time, a pain that seemed to pierce to the very marrow of her bones as she lay down at night.

Without food, she couldn't sleep. She felt nauseated, but continued fasting through the final day. She was thrilled when the Council passed a specific condemnation against atomic war. It stated: "Every act of war directed to the indiscriminate destruction of whole cities or vast areas with their inhabitants is a crime against God and humanity, which merits firm and unequivocal condemnation." The Council also, for the first time, supported conscientious objectors and their refusal to take part in wars they thought were morally wrong. Furthermore, the Catholic Worker movement itself was acknowledged for its contributions to the Council.

Soon after her return, however, a tragedy took place involving the New York Worker house. It brought condemnation on the Catholic Worker movement and much bad publicity.

Roger LaPorte was a young man who stayed regularly at the Chrystie Street house. In protest of the Vietnam War, he dowsed his clothes with gasoline, then set himself on fire in front of the United Nations. In the ambulance on the way to the hospital, LaPorte whispered, "I am a Catholic Worker. I did this to protest the Vietnam War." He died the next day.

The story made the front page of every paper, many with photos of LaPorte's burning body. TV newscasters featured films of the tragic scene. But instead of bringing followers to the cause of peace, the young protester's fiery death brought Dorothy reproach from all sides. To most people Dorothy Day *was* the Catholic Worker movement, and she was blamed by many for LaPorte's suicide. Dorothy was deeply hurt by the cruel accusations hurled her way. She had never even met LaPorte. Also, all her speeches, books, and articles—as well as everything she did and said—affirmed how strongly she valued human life. She had never condoned throwing life away for any cause.

In 1967, Dorothy visited Rome again to attend the International Congress of the Laity. This time she was recognized everywhere and treated as an honored guest. She was even invited to receive communion personally from Pope Paul VI, who had succeeded John XXIII. This special moment touched her deeply. Disturbed by young Americans fighting and dying in the Vietnam War, Dorothy offered her communion for them, particularly for the many conscientious objectors sentenced to prison.

Another high point of that 1967 trip was meeting Cardinal Leo Suenens of Belgium. The Cardinal invited Dorothy to his villa on a hilltop overlooking the Eternal City. There she addressed a group of clergy and lay leaders on the dignity of the human person.

Eventually her schedule and her age caught up with her, and her once-robust health began to disappear.

Doctors had diagnosed her swollen ankles and shortness of breath as congestive heart failure. At first she saw the diagnosis as a death sentence. But with medication to hold the disease in check, she resumed her regular busy schedule. This included her prayer routine of Mass, the rosary, the Psalms, and prayer before the Reserved Sacrament; her work routine of writing, serving the poor, running the Worker houses, and participating in protests; and her personal enjoyments as mother and grandmother.

CHAPTER ELEVEN

A PEACEFUL END

Time was running out for Dorothy Day. Once vigorous and active, she no longer had the strength to serve others, travel, or give speeches. One last effort would be a book of spiritual musings compiled from her diary and retreat notes. This she titled *All Is Grace* and began it before Lent in 1973. However, the final manuscript was not published until 1987, seven years after her death, appearing under the name of her longtime friend, William D. Miller, whom she had asked to put her notes in order.

Also in 1973, Dorothy bought a former music school on East Third Street to house the many homeless "bag ladies" roaming New York's streets. She named the three connecting buildings Maryhouse, and there she spent her final years.

Dorothy turned over the daily management of *The Catholic Worker* to a younger woman, but continued the editorship and wrote her column, "On Pilgrimage," to the end. However, shortness of breath and a crippling weakness kept her confined to her second story-room. Maryhouse had a chapel where Mass was celebrated twice a week. When she was too weak to go downstairs, a priest brought the Eucharist to her.

In addition to heart trouble, Dorothy suffered from arthritis in her knees. Yet in the summer of 1973 she flew to California to join union leader Cesar Chavez in a march with his United Farm Workers. Migrant workers and their supporters walked through the San Joaquin Valley in a protest against the Teamsters Union, which had undercut their efforts by signing their own, more favorable deal with grape growers. Thousands of arrests, beatings, shootings, and even murders of farm workers had already marked the protest, which had started that spring.

Wearing a broad-brimmed hat to protect her from the sun, and using a cane for support, Dorothy walked beside Chavez in the shimmery August heat. That day Dorothy, Chavez, and over a hundred protesters were arrested and jailed. Her short time in custody brought the Farm Workers Union a great deal of attention and nationwide support. The publicity also showed an aging activist still ready to go to prison for a worthy cause.

Admiration for Dorothy grew. She was referred to as that "saintly woman" in article after article. She hated being called a "saint." It embarrassed her, yet at the same time she thought the word made her seem harmless. She would growl at the offender, "Don't call me a saint, I don't want to be dismissed so easily."

In 1975 Dorothy Day received the Gandhi Award, given to honor those who worked for peace through nonviolent means. It was presented to her at the Unitarian Church on Park Avenue. As this was only a taxi ride away from Maryhouse, she was able to attend. In addition, she was awarded the Laetere Medal by Notre

Dame University. Other universities and many peace and religious organizations wanted to honor Dorothy as well during her last decade. However, they not only requested that she attend when they bestowed the degree or medal, they also expected the increasingly frail woman to give an acceptance speech. Once robust and tireless, Dorothy had become too weak to travel or to sit through long, tiring ceremonies. She declined most all of these requests.

One honor she gladly accepted. A long, black limousine pulled up to the First Street house carrying New York's Cardinal Terrence Cooke. Stepping out of the car, he presented Dorothy with a greeting from Pope Paul VI on her eightieth birthday. On that occasion, she was feted in many other ways. A two-day celebration was held in her honor at Marquette University. The festivities began with a High Mass in the Gesu Chapel. Friends who had been part of the Catholic Worker movement came from near and far to celebrate Dorothy's life and work.

After her eightieth birthday, Dorothy, who once traveled the world, was forced to stay at home. Instead, others came to her. One last visit was from Cesar Chavez, another was from Mother Teresa. As her health failed, Dorothy spent more and more time in her room. She had difficulty breathing, her appetite disappeared, and she lost weight.

Yet nothing stopped her from answering the daily pile of mail. She wrote regularly to her beloved sister, Della, reminiscing about their childhood, their favorite books, their playmates. She also continued to correspond with several longtime friends. One was Sister

Peter Claver whom she had known since 1933. Another was Stanley Vishnewski, who had joined the Worker movement when he was seventeen and never left, living in the New York house. Gentle, humble, and always ready with a joke, after almost half a century as a Catholic Worker, Stanley still protested, "I'm just trying it out."

But Dorothy's loved ones were aging along with her. Her parents were already long dead, then Stanley died in 1979, and Della in 1980. Taking their place were grandchildren and even great-grandchildren. Tamar brought them to Maryhouse for visits, while Forster Batterham, Tamar's father, phoned every day. But for the most part, Dorothy's last three years were a time of slowing down, preparing her soul for heaven.

Both Catholic and secular publications eulogized her while she was still alive, as her legacy was considerable. She had dedicated her life to hands-on care of the poor, co-founded the Catholic Worker movement, popularized retreats, and authored six books.

Under Peter Maurin's guidance, Dorothy Day had helped introduce a new style of active lay Catholicism to America. Her book *The Long Loneliness* has never been out of print since its publication in 1952. Through *The Catholic Worker* she brought many social causes to the attention of readers everywhere. She ran the paper herself for forty-seven years, with its monthly circulation averaging 100,000 copies. The Catholic Worker movement spread via its publication to inspire young men and women to open their homes and hearts in hospitality for all, and to love and care for the needy.

To many people Dorothy Day was *the* leading Catholic layperson of the twentieth century. Even so, she still had detractors. Conservatives were uneasy with her personal past and her political leanings, and were shocked by her forwardness. At the same time, liberals were embarrassed that she was so old-fashioned. She refused to call priests by their first names, preferring to see them in clerical collars rather than sport shirts, and she favored traditional religious practices. Also, despite of—or perhaps *because* of—her own experience, she frowned on the sexual freedoms taken for granted in these modern times.

In 1980 Tamar moved with her children from Vermont to the city to make her mother's last days more comfortable. The afternoon of November 29, 1980, she was visiting Dorothy at Maryhouse. Dorothy lay quietly as Tamar clung tightly to her hand. Suddenly that worn hand went limp. Dorothy Day was gone. Her passing was quick and free of pain. For a few minutes Tamar sat beside her mother, weeping softly, then she went downstairs to announce to the household that their beloved founder had died.

Dorothy's entire wardrobe consisted of secondhand clothes from the Worker's free clothing store. Tamar picked out a blue and white checked dress for the funeral. Dorothy lay before the altar at Maryhouse in a simple pine casket that had been handmade by a worker. Her body appeared thin and frail. But her strong face still reflected its youthful beauty. A single rose adorned her casket; a cross stood above.

A long line of visitors came to pay their respects and pray beside the woman they considered a saint.

Hundreds came to the small chapel to say a final goodbye—Jews, Catholics, Protestants, the rich and the shabby, the well known and the unknown.

The funeral Mass was held December 2 at 11 A.M. in the nearby Church of the Nativity. Dorothy's grandchildren acted as pallbearers, carrying the plain coffin the half block to the church. Cardinal Cooke met the procession at the church door and blessed the body in its pine box.

Dorothy had always loved Staten Island. She had lived there happily with Forster. Tamar had been conceived and baptized there. It was the fitting place for her burial. The simple coffin was lowered into a donated grave in Resurrection Cemetery, close to the site of Dorothy's cottage during the 1920s. A plain granite stone was placed over the grave. It bore the inscription: Dorothy Day, November 8, 1897—November 29, 1980. Above those words was engraved a loaf of bread and two fish.

After Dorothy Day's death, her fame did not end; rather, it grew. Biographies have been written about her; whole issues of magazines have been devoted to her. *The Long Loneliness* is considered one of the major religious books of the twentieth century. College symposiums have brought together noted people to speak about her and her work. And the question keeps arising: Was Dorothy Day a saint? More and more people say, "Yes."

CHAPTER TWELVE

DOROTHY DAY'S SPIRITUALITY

Thousands of social workers devote their lives to helping the poor and the dysfunctional. Hordes of idealists have marched in support of causes, some even dying for those causes. That doesn't necessarily make them saints. What made Dorothy Day different? In addition to her devoted service to the destitute on skid row and the courageous support of her ideals, she had a relationship with God that grew ever closer and stronger throughout the years. She was an inspiration to countless Catholics who read and acted upon her books and articles. Priests and lay people alike came to her for spiritual advice.

Dorothy's spiritual pilgrimage began long before she entered the Catholic Church. In her radical days as a teenager at the University of Illinois, she was influenced by the novels of Russian Orthodox writer Fyodor Dostoevsky. Father Zossima, a character in Dostoevsky's novel *The Brothers Karamazov*, expressed the goodness possible in humanity. Over the years Dorothy often quoted Father Zossima: "Love in action is a harsh and dreadful thing." And the Grand Inquisitor in the same book declared that the ultimate craving of every human is a final unity of all. Dorothy saw that as a call to community, the very theme that motivated her through most of the twentieth century.

After her conversion, she drifted spiritually, unsure of what God wanted her to do. She moved around the country, trying different jobs, writing first a novel based on her youth, then a play comparing Communism and Christianity, then another novel. She was searching for her purpose in life, the "Hound of Heaven" hard at her heels, when Peter Maurin finally appeared in her tenement kitchen and pointed her toward a new path, a new way of Catholicism: community, simplicity, and love.

The period that changed Dorothy the most and became a deep spiritual awakening, a time she called her "luminous years," was the result of a series of silent retreats held in the 1940s. It all began when Sister Peter Claver, whom Dorothy first met on Staten Island in the twenties, had received retreat notes taken by a Father Egan. He had made the notes during an eight-day retreat for priests in Baltimore, led by a prayerful Canadian Jesuit, Father Onesimus Lacouture. The retreat had been filled with joy and enthusiasm. Wanting to share his amazing experience, Father Egan sent his notes to Sister Peter Claver and told her she should read them before the Blessed Sacrament in an attitude of prayer. Then Sister gave the notes to Dorothy with the same instructions. Dorothy was very moved by what she read.

She herself could not attend the retreats led by Father Lacouture, as they were only offered to ordained priests, so she asked Sister Peter Claver, "Where can I find priests who are conducting such retreats?" Fortunately, the sister had an answer. Father John Hugo in Oakmont, a suburb of Pittsburgh, was offering the same kind of program for the laity, based on what he had absorbed during his own experience of the Lacouture retreats.

Outwardly, Father Hugo's career as a priest seemed ordinary: years as a teacher, an assistant pastor at various parishes, later a chaplain at a prison, then finally a pastor of a new parish near Pittsburgh. But inwardly he had a firmness and thirst for certitude that did not allow him to take the easy, comfortable path. For him, the very purpose of priesthood was to change people's lives, but so many priests did not want to pay the price to do it, and that was to become saints themselves.

What led him on his difficult path was the spiritual depth he gained from Father Lacouture's retreats. It was there that he decided to spend the rest of his life sharing the magnificent vision of the Christian life Lacouture revealed. This same vision was what he presented at the retreat Dorothy Day attended and where she first met him. Dorothy saw it as a "radical" Christianity, with its emphasis on the spirituality of St. John of the Cross requiring detachment from those impulses for power and possession. Instead, this Christianity led to training oneself to always prefer not what was easiest, but what was hardest, to allow oneself to be stripped of everything the world could offer, and to be poor for Christ's sake.

The exultation of the power of love was one of the continuing principles of the retreat. "In the evening of life we shall be judged by love," wrote St. John of the Cross. At the conclusion of this retreat, Dorothy began her own "ascent" to a new, higher level of life. And afterwards, she told Sister Peter Claver, "At last I have found what I was looking for when I left my Communist friends and became a Catholic."

What Dorothy gained from the retreat, and the notes she took of it, became her main source of spiritual energy the remainder of her life. It was due to this that she also organized regular retreats at the Worker's farm in Easton. These were conducted by Father Hugo, each one lasting a week, running from 1940 through 1949.

Father Hugo continued to influence Dorothy as spiritual director and confessor for the rest of her life. She wrote to her fellow Workers, "We must drop everything and spend one week listening to our Lord, who will speak only if we keep silent."

Dorothy was also inspired by contemplating nature. The beauty of the sea and the shore, the wind and the waves, the tide, the gulls, the seaweed and shells, all gave testimony of a creator, a Father Almighty, who was made known to us by his Son, Jesus. Dorothy felt that we had to be converted "step by step, little by little" and that the beauty of the world was a "natural" path to this.

After her conversion, she immersed herself in prayer and the sacraments. She read the Bible in all the new translations then available. She read the daily offices—Matins and Lauds, which consist mostly of psalms. One time, when she was in jail for refusing to take shelter during an air-raid drill, her roommate, a drug addict, remarked, "When I wake up in the morning you are reading that little book, and when I go to sleep at night, you are still reading it. Me, the first and last thing I think about is when I get out of here I'll 'get me a fix.'" Dorothy also attended daily Mass whenever possible. She considered the Mass to be glorious. Only its constant reassurance helped her dare to write or speak or work for the poor and for peace.

The virtues Dorothy Day most admired were fidelity and constancy. Her life was a showcase of those virtues. She was faithful and constant in her life of prayer, in her service to the poor, and in her support of world peace.

Another aspect of her spiritually was her kinship with St. Thérèse de Lisieux, better known as "The Little Flower." This popular French saint, who was pampered and spoiled as a child, entered the Carmelite Order when she was only sixteen and died at age twenty-four of tuberculosis. During her very short life she developed a method of holiness for ordinary people, a method so full of spiritual wisdom that she was canonized in 1924, only twenty-eight years after her death. A few decades afterwards she was declared a "Doctor of the Church." St. Thérèse described this method in the spiritual diary she kept during the last years of her life. It was published after her death as *The Story of a Soul.*

Dorothy was so moved by St. Thérèse's writings that she decided to write a biography of the Carmelite saint; it was published in 1960. In her autobiography, St. Thérèse told of her "little way" to sanctity. Dorothy took this as her own way to holiness. We are all called to be saints, she thought, not called to do the extraordinary. If holiness depended on doing the extraordinary, there would be few saints. Dorothy's deepest insight into Thérèse was the result of the year she spent in a convent of Dominican Sisters on Long Island, living in solitude and silence. That period of time helped her better understand the greatness of Thérèse, and how everything came from "doing nothing."

Dorothy submerged herself in prayer on her path to holiness. The purpose of prayer, she thought, was not to ask for "things" but to ask for grace, the grace to let Christ grow in us. We are not holy, she reasoned, because we don't ask for holiness. If we ask in prayer for holiness, and if we pray that our whole lives are used to promote God's glory and to love Christ in others, then all of us will be saints.

One of the most striking things about Dorothy Day was the simplicity of her life. She was a successful journalist and published author who was regarded with awe by millions, even by celebrities. Yet she continued to live with and among the poor, who were often uneducated, disturbed, unwashed street people who came to Worker houses expecting, even demanding, food and shelter. She responded to their needs with dedicated love, always giving, never taking. She wore the same kinds of used clothing they might wear, selected from a roomful of dresses, suits, and shoes that had been donated to the indigents. She never owned more than three pairs of secondhand socks, and even these she patched and darned until they disintegrated. She also took her meals with the Worker's "guests," eating the same leftovers and castoffs donated by grocery stores and restaurants. These meals she considered sacred because Jesus had come to us as food.

Many times Dorothy was accused of being naive, accepting the stories the down-and-outers offered her as excuses. Her detractors claimed that these poor people were failures who got what they deserved. But

she refused to waste time over abstractions, instead focusing on real people and their real immediate needs. In this way, her simplicity and deliberate child-likeness were not only revealed in her lifestyle, but in her solutions to problems. She did not concern herself with the how's and why's of a person's poverty, only with what they needed at the moment. In this way she refused to dismiss the poor as undeserving of unconditional love and mercy.

She was much drawn to St. Joseph, who raised Jesus and instilled in Our Savior many of his own gentle qualities. Dorothy named the first Worker house for this gentle, simple father guide. Whenever the house needed food or money, or a major decision needed to be made, Dorothy would go to St. Joseph and lay her request before him. St. Joseph always "came through," often providing the exact sum needed to acquire a new farm or building. The saint's generosity naturally increased her abiding faith in him.

Dorothy never had a home of her own other than the cottage on Staten Island. She was content to live in any unneeded room in a Worker tenement. She was free of the material requirements of today. She never used for herself any of the substantial donations that came in through *The Catholic Worker*, and the only money she directly earned—royalties from her books—she used to educate and support her daughter, Tamar.

Dorothy generally traveled by bus, the transportation of America's poor. At various times she used donated cars to transport Workers or "guests" to the distant farms owned by the Catholic Worker movement. But she preferred buses, which allowed her long hours to pray or read, usually books by or about saints. She was daily inspired by those holy men and women who showed us the way. Her favorite saints were Teresa of Avila, St. John of the Cross, and of course St. Thérèse de Lisieux. What they discovered in their own life of prayer fostered Dorothy's growth in holiness.

Naturally Dorothy Day had failings and weaknesses, like every human. But what makes her stand out from the "cloud of witnesses" in our modern, hectic world, was her goodness and her all-encompassing care for humanity. Her life can be summed up in the words of Father Hugo, her spiritual advisor, "Love is the measure. Everything Dorothy did was in the name of love."

Chapter Thirteen

The World Passes Judgment

A rebel in her youth, a radical activist in her middle years, and a spiritual guide in her old age, Dorothy Day was always a leader, pointing Catholics toward action and holiness through the example of her own life. Her turbulent past has frequently been compared to that of St. Augustine, who in his wild youth prayed for God to make him good, but not just yet. But Augustine wasn't under the 24/7 scrutiny of modern media, and today it is his holiness that is largely remembered, not his many human failings.

Cardinal John O'Connor of the Archdiocese of New York addressed the matter of Day's past directly in his letter to the Holy See initiating the process of canonization. He said that her conversion from such a youth "demonstrates the mercy of God" and that it "should not preclude her cause but intensify it."[1]

Despite her well-known past, Dorothy Day was often declared a saint even during her lifetime. As early as 1952, Dwight Macdonald wrote in his *New Yorker* profile of her, "Many people think Dorothy Day is a saint and that someday she will be canonized."[2]

Read Bain—professor of sociology, editor of *Humanist Magazine*, and for decades a correspondent of

Day's—wrote to her directly: "I am more certain you will eventually become a saint." He told her, "You are on the right track because you have struck at the economic inequalities and cruel denial of life values that have grown up within modern capitalism." And in his magazine, he wrote, "I still say Dorothy Day is headed for sainthood. If I were Pope, I would canonize her."[3]

Only three years after her death the Claretian Fathers began the initial work that would eventually lead to the canonization process. Why the Claretians? It is an order devoted to promoting social justice. It also has a publishing apostolate that includes two magazines, *U.S. Catholic* and *Salt.*

Diocesan priest Father Henry Fehren had already written an article for the Claretians, published in *Salt* the year before, in which he proposed, "Let's canonize Dorothy Day as a saint for our time." He continued, "In the past we thought of saints as more than human. But Dorothy lived in our age, with the same fears, weaknesses, doubts, and problems that we all have. We need her for a realistic ideal."[4] Now *Salt* issued a plea for readers to mail in personal accounts of Dorothy's sanctity. Thousands of touching letters arrived in response, many from down-and-outers she had helped, and others from friends and workers who knew her intimately. All praised Dorothy, though some protested that she herself would not want to be called a saint. For fifteen years, the Claretians compiled material, and then they shipped it off to Cardinal John O'Connor. They thought Day's cause should spring from New York, the city where Dorothy was born and spent most of her life.

The Claretians asked that O'Connor use the centenary of her birth, 1997, to officially open her cause for canonization. The cardinal responded. In the homily he preached November 9, 1997, in St. Patrick's Cathedral, O'Connor asked, "What was there about Dorothy Day to make such an appeal? Perhaps because she was so much like the rest of us in her ordinariness. In her lifetime there were no miracles recounted. She was just 'good.'" Following the sermon, Cardinal O'Connor called two meetings of Day's friends and colleagues. He wanted to listen personally to people who had known Dorothy Day firsthand and had intimate knowledge of her life.

George Horton was in charge of the Dorothy Day cause for the Archdiocese of New York. In the two meetings with Day's friends and colleagues, Horton said there was a feeling of spirit he had rarely felt before, a feeling that these people had been in the presence of someone special. Just how special is evident from the many praises and testimonials written about this most extraordinary woman.

Robert Ellsberg, noted author and one-time editor of *The Catholic Worker*, explained that Day rediscovered the gospel challenge of finding Christ in the poor. Ellsberg believes that "Dorothy Day is an authentic saint who spoke to the demands of our times."[5]

Author Anne Fremantle, a frequent visitor to New York's Worker houses, wrote in an issue of *America*, devoted entirely to Dorothy Day on the occasion of her seventy-fifth birthday, "She is the most unsentimental of saints and calls life as it is. Dorothy points out, 'If you will to love someone, you soon do. You will to love this cranky old man, and someday you do. It all depends on how hard you try.' No one ever tried harder than Dorothy. 'She loved enough' are perhaps the only words adequate to describe her."[6]

Just one month after her death, David O'Brien wrote in *Commonweal*, "She was the most significant, interesting, influential person in the history of American Catholicism." O'Brien concluded, "The chief gift of Dorothy Day and the Catholic Worker, to both church and society, was the creation of a community from which it is practically impossible to be expelled."[7]

Some years later, another *Commonweal* article, this one written by Patrick Jordan, emphasized Dorothy's unending work for peace and her insistence on nonviolence. She had protested all U.S. military involvement, from World War I through Vietnam, describing war as "simply murder wrapped up in flags."[8]

Jim Forest, Dorothy Day's best-known biographer, was only twenty when he first met her at the Catholic Worker's farm on Staten Island. The next twenty years she scolded and encouraged him on a daily basis, as he wrote for and eventually edited *The Catholic Worker*. Speaking at Marquette University on the centenary of her birth, he explained how central to her life was the idea of hospitality. Hospitality was simply the practice of God's mercy, especially toward the stranger, the poor, and the marginalized, but through these "simple actions" we learn to see the face of Christ. Forest concluded his remarks by saying that we remember Dorothy Day "as a saint, if by the word 'Saint' we mean a person who helps us see, both by precept and example, what it means to follow Christ."[9]

Friends and coworkers are not the only ones to call Dorothy a saint.

Newsweek displayed a photo of Dorothy late in life in her usual second-hand dress, a scarf covering her snow-white hair. The accompanying article stated, "Dorothy Day is on her way to canonization twenty years after her death. At the urging of Cardinal John O'Connor, once reluctant to push her cause, the Vatican opened the process last week."[10] In the same issue was another article, written by Lutheran minister Martin Marty. Marty stated, "Most of the two billion Christians of today see in the cross and God's reconciling activity a divine, empowering love. They have seen in the reconciling Christ an empowering of strong reconcilers—Martin Luther King, Pope John XXIII, Dorothy Day, Desmond Tutu, and so many unknown fighters against abuse."[11]

Yet despite her unquestioned holiness and the reverence she inspires in her admirers, Day proves a refreshing contrast to the stereotypical meek and unassuming female saint. Michael Harrington, a Catholic Worker alumnus, recalled his years at the Worker in the early fifties: "Whenever we had to make a decision, we had a completely democratic discussion and then Dorothy made up her mind."[12]

An editorial in *The Progressive* noted: "Dorothy Day deserved to be called a saint, but it was not a sentiment she would have appreciated. Day devoted her life to achieving a peaceful and just world. She didn't embrace peace and justice as a goal, or a cause or a vocation. She lived peace and justice and she brooked no compromise."[13]

In March of 2000, Dorothy Day was declared a "Servant of God," meaning the Vatican formally accepted Cardinal O'Connor's request that the canonization process be started. This is just the first step on the very long road to sainthood. The Congregation for the Causes of Saints is now hard at work digging through the flood of words written by Day herself, as well as the millions written about her.

Becoming a Servant of God offers no guarantee; in fact, most candidates that are proposed for formal sainthood are not accepted. Meanwhile Dorothy Day is honored by the people as a saint of the twentieth century, a saint of the bum, the homeless, the prostitute, the dirty, the unwanted, the drunk, and the hopeless.

Her trademark was simplicity, expressed through a lifetime of voluntary poverty. Yet she was also defiant, always the anarchist in disguise, never voting, never paying income taxes, never owning a social security card, and never belonging to a political party.

Was her saintliness something anyone could copy, try to aim for? Hundreds of young men and women flocked to her farms and houses of hospitality, working as volunteers, sharing their food, their clothing, and even their beds with the poor and homeless. If a saint is a beacon of light attracting and guiding other Christians, certainly this selfless, giving woman was a saint. If a saint shows the glory and love of God through her life, then surely Dorothy Day was a saint. But at the same time, she saw sainthood as a goal for *everyone,* and put it in terms of her constant struggle for peace: "We are called to be saints...Nothing less will work. Nothing less is powerful enough to combat war...."[14]

But she was never a plaster saint, set apart from other human beings, as this final little story signifies.

One time, when Dorothy Day was in her seventies, she went to visit a distant Worker house only to find a little boy weeping copiously. When asked why he was crying, the child replied, "All day everyone has been so excited, saying, 'Dorothy Day is coming! Dorothy Day is coming!' Now she's here and she's nothing but an old woman." No doubt she reached down and wiped away his tears.

NOTES

1. John Cardinal O'Connor, "Dorothy Day Sainthood Cause Begins," *Catholic New York*, March 16, 2000.

2. Dwight Macdonald, "Profile" of Dorothy Day, Part One, *The New Yorker*, October 4, 1952, 37.

3. The Bain quotes are all cited in *Dorothy Day: A Biography* by William D. Miller, San Francisco: Harper & Row, 1982, 380–81.

4. The description of the Claretians' efforts, Cardinal O'Connor's homily on Day, and the two meetings with those who knew her are from "The Reluctant Saint" by T. Wright Townsend, *Chicago Tribune Magazine*, December 26, 1999, 10+.

5. Robert Ellsberg, lecture on Dorothy Day, given on the centenary of her birth, New York University, November 8, 1997. The lecture is quoted in full on the Catholic Worker Movement website, www.catholicworker.org/dorothyday/canonizationtext.cfm? Number=33.

6. Anne Fremantle, "Dorothy Day and the Catholic Worker Movement," *America*, November 11, 1972, 376–77. Eleven other authors contributed to the all-Day issue.

7. David O'Brien, *Commonweal*, December 19, 1980.

8. Patrick Jordan, "Dorothy Day: Still a Radical," *Commonweal*, November 29, 1985, 29.

9. Jim Forest, "The Trouble with Saint Dorothy," *U.S. Catholic*, November 1997.

10. *Newsweek*, March 27, 2000, 4.

11. Martin Marty, "The Long Road to Reconciliation," *Newsweek*, March 27, 2000, 61.

12. Michael Harrington, quoted in "Saint Dorothy?" *The Nation*, May 1, 2000, 7.

13. *The Progressive,* 1994.

14. Dorothy Day, writing in *The Catholic Worker,* April 1958; quoted in "Seminarian Discovers Dorothy Day" by Jose Rueda, *Houston Catholic Worker,* Vol. XXIII, No. 2, March–April 2003.

References

Books

Day, Dorothy. *The Long Loneliness*. Harper and Brothers: New York, 1952.

——. *The Eleventh Virgin*. Albert and Charles Boni: New York, 1924.

——. *From Union Square to Rome*. Preservation of the Faith Press: Silver Spring, Maryland, 1938.

Ellsberg, Robert, and Tamar Hennessy. *By Little and By Little*, the selected writings of Dorothy Day. Alfred A. Knopf, New York, 1983.

Forest, Jim. *Love Is the Measure: A Biography of Dorothy Day*. Paulist Press: New York, 1986.

Gay, Kathleen and Marilen. *Heroes of Conscience: A Biographical Dictionary*, 1996.

Kent, Deborah. *Dorothy Day: Friend to the Forgotten*. William B. Erdmans: Grand Rapids, Michigan, 1996.

Miller, William D. *All Is Grace: The Spirituality of Dorothy Day*. Doubleday: New York, 1987.

——. *Dorothy Day: A Biography*. Harper and Row: San Francisco, 1982.

Articles about Dorothy Day

Cornell, Tom. "A Brief Introduction to the Catholic Worker Movement," April 10, 1997. Posted on the Catholic Worker website, http://www.catholicworker.com/cwo010.htm

Coy, Patrick G. "Dorothy Day, Wondering at Her Simplicity." *Fellowship Magazine*, November/December, 1998.

DOROTHY DAY

Ellsberg, Robert. "Dorothy Day." Lecture on Centenary, New York University, given November 8, 1997. Posted at the Catholic Worker website, www.catholicworker.org/dorothyday/canonizationtext.cfm?Number=33.

Jordan, Patrick. "Dorothy Day: Still a Radical." *Commonweal*, November 29, 1985, 29.

Macdonald, Dwight. "Profile on Dorothy Day." *The New Yorker*, part one, October 4, 1952; part two, October 11, 1952.

O'Connor, Cardinal John. Homily on the "Idea of Sainthood and Dorothy Day," given November 9, 1997.

Townsend, T. Wright. "The Reluctant Saint." *Chicago Tribune*, December 26, 1999.

Various authors. "Dorothy Day and the Catholic Worker Movement," *America*, November 11, 1972.

———. "100 Christian Books of the Century: *The Long Loneliness* by Dorothy Day." *Christianity Today*, April 1999.

———. "The Case for Saint Dorothy." *Newsweek*, March 27, 2000.

———. *The Catholic Worker*, May 2000.

———. "Saint Dorothy?" *The Nation*, May 1, 2000.

———. Review of *The Life You Save May Be Your Own* by Paul Elie. *Time*, April 14, 2003.

Websites on Dorothy Day and the Catholic Worker Movement

The Catholic Worker Movement homepage:
www.catholicworker.org

Dorothy Day and Catholic Worker Special Collection, archived at Marquette University:
http://www.marquette.edu/library/collections/archives/day.html

"Dorothy Day and the Staten Island Years," a special photo exhibit from Marquette University, online at:
http://www.marquette.edu/library/collections/archives/projects/DDE/page01.html